text, lies, & videotape

text, lies, & videotape

stories about life, literacy, & learning

Patrick Shannon

HEINEMANN
Portsmouth, NH

Heinemann
A division of Reed Elsevier Inc.
361 Hanover Street
Portsmouth, NH 03801-3912

Offices and agents throughout the world

Every effort has been made to contact the copyright holders and students for permission to reprint borrowed material. We regret any oversights that may have occurred and would be happy to rectify them in future printings of this work.

Library of Congress Cataloging-in-Publication Data
Shannon, Patrick, 1951–
    Text, lies & videotape : stories about life, literacy, & learning
Patrick Shannon.
        p.   cm.
    Includes bibliographical references.
    ISBN 0-435-08120-9
    1. Literacy—Social aspects—United States.   2. Language arts—
Social aspects—United States.   3. Critical pedagogy—United
States.   I. Title.
    LC151.S43   1995
    302.2'244—dc20

                                                                                            95-1840
                                                                                            CIP

Editor: Cheryl Kimball
Production: Renée M. Nicholls
Cover Design: Barbara Werden
Cover Photo: Tim Nicholls

Printed in the United States of America on acid-free paper
99 98 97 96 95 VB 1 2 3 4 5 6

For my mother,
Mary R. Shannon

Contents

Preface

Boyd Beck was the principal of the junior high school I attended in 1963. He was a strawberry blond with freckles and baggy suits that seemed gray from age. He smelled of tobacco always, although smoking was prohibited for junior high school students. Our school had many rules about deportment, property, and dress. To my knowledge these rules were not committed to print anywhere, but everyone knew "the school rules" and that they were about respect and civility.

I first came in contact with Mr. Beck on the third day of school when I took strike three in the dress code for not wearing pants sufficiently loose to drop a Ping-Pong ball down the leg. My pants caused Mabel Fleming, my homeroom and English teacher, no end of concern. On the first day of school, she noticed that my chinos were too tight and called me to the front of the room to give me the Ping-Pong ball test. Apparently all teachers had such balls in their desk drawers for such occasions.

I failed the Ping-Pong ball test on that day, day two, and day three, despite a note to my mother. After the third failure, I was sent to sit on "the bad boy's bench" (there was no bad girl's bench) and to see Mr. Beck. After a few brief words about school rules, he paddled me with the type of paddle used in fraternity hazings at the time. He paddled me with even fewer words the next day and the day after. No notes went home to my mother from his office. I told her nothing except that I was handling the situation.

On the following Monday, I failed the Ping-Pong ball test again. Curiously, Miss Fleming gave me the test each day even though it should have been clear to all that I had only two pairs of pants to wear to school. Apparently tired of paddling me, Mr. Beck decided to take a more drastic step. He threatened that if I did not pass the dress code the next day, I would be assigned to section 9 for my classes.

Our junior high was tracked by ability and students were assigned to teachers and courses only by section. In order to avoid the stigma of a numbering system, the top third of our class was cleverly assigned to sections 1, 2, and 10; the middle third to sections 3, 4, and 5; and the bottom third to sections 6, 7, and 8. Section 9 was the equivalent of what is now called a special education class. It had only two academic classes, mathematics and English, along with wood shop, metal shop, gym, and home economics.

On the seventh day of school, I was transferred to section 9, where I was introduced to the other side—the north side— of the railroad tracks in my home town: Mike Granicio, Bernadette Ducci, Mike Donevio, Steve Bacco, Nicky Crosetti, Rocko Crosetti (Nicky's older brother), Rose Crosetti (Nicky's and Rocko's cousin), Anita Risio, John Bessimi, and others. I learned much from these individuals during the two weeks I spent in section 9. I learned whose house to visit for the best spaghetti I will ever eat; how to make money after school by carrying groceries for everyone's grandmother from the corner market; and some things about sex that my friends on the south side thought I was making up.

From this experience I also learned much more. Because I was never given the Ping-Pong ball test after the seventh day and I was only "sentenced" to section 9 for two weeks, I learned that school rules were more about control of students' minds and bodies than about promoting an effective learning environment or developing civility or civic mindedness. Enforcement of those rules was to come from public humiliation, physical pain, and academic and social segregation. All of this because I had fat legs.

Moreover, I learned that the Shannons, the Turners, the Treadways, the Smalls, the Bennetts, and the Carsons were treated differently at school (and in town) than the Nittis, Diriscos, and the D'Gemblardinos. The latter group wasn't challenged at school or given much opportunity to demonstrate its abilities. They were the sons and daughters of workers at the can factory, the car shops, or the piano works. Mr. Beck and the teachers assigned primarily working-class Italians and some farm kids to sections 6, 7, and 8 and exclusively to section 9. Mr. Beck could think of nothing worse for an apparently defiant adolescent than to send him to "the hell of section 9." In short, I learned that schooling is not meant to be the same for all social groups.

I start with this story over thirty years later because, unfortunately, the lessons I learned are still true about schooling—rules are often arbitrary, public humiliation is often used to control students, and tracking is still widespread, often socially biased, and always artificial. Moreover, I start with a story because stories are important to people, politics, and education. Stories are how people make sense of themselves and their worlds. In young children's spontaneous stories that they act out as they play, we can see how they believe people relate to one another, who they hope to become, and how they will behave. We can see adolescents play roles in their own and other people's stories in order to figure out where they fit into their ever-expanding worlds. As adults, the true and imaginary stories we wish to tell and believe suggest what we value most in this world. In a real sense, stories make people.

For this reason, stories are political. Whose stories get told? What can these stories mean? Who benefits from their telling? These are political questions because they address the ways in which people's identities—their beliefs, attitudes, and values—are created and maintained. These identities determine how we live together in and out of schools as much as school rules or governmental laws. For example, during the 1980s, many Americans believed the story of the Reagan administration's campaign, "Morning in America," which privileged some stories and people over others.

Although they are not alone, teachers and schools are in the identity creation business. That's why there are so many different groups vying for control of schools and school curricula. Business executives and government officials want "standards" in order to make the American economy competitive and second to none. Advocacy groups led by Ralph Nader and the National Association of Education Activists want "civics for democracy" in schools in order that the majority of America will reinvest themselves in America. Psychologists such as Lauren Resnick, James Comer, and Robert Slavin want schools to be "effective" for all students. Teachers' groups such as the Whole Language Umbrella and the National Association for the Education of Young Children want schools to be humane places where students can "reach their potential." Each group tells its story compellingly; each claims the patriotic and democratic center for itself. And each is a political story.

Stories set parameters for our thinking as we blend the stories we've read, heard, or seen with the events in our lives that also seem to come to us as stories. That is, we read and write our lives as if they were texts and we negotiate meaning from and with those texts. Negotiation is necessary because meaning is neither exclusively in the text nor in our heads. Rather, meaning comes from our consideration of texts by using our heads at a particular time in a certain place. And texts are more than just written language on paper or screen. Texts are the symbols that surround us in our daily lives that we must interpret for the meaning in our lives. My story of my initiation into junior high school is a text of which I was and am both a reader through my interpretations of the symbols—the pants, the paddle, and the tracking—and a writer through my involvement, actions, and retellings. I read and write the story quite differently than I did at that time, and I'm sure that Mr. Beck and Miss Fleming were readers and writers of this text also—with different negotiated meanings.

My ability to negotiate meaning from texts makes me literate. My ability to use those negotiated meanings in order to make sense of my life, history, and culture; to make connections between my life and those of others; and to take action upon what I learn about myself and the world gives me some power and enables me to have some control over my life. This literacy empowers me to read and write the past, the present, and the future—it offers me freedom to explore and act.

The film *sex, lies, and videotape* (1991, Columbia Tristar) is about this sense of literacy. Its characters reread the texts of their past in order to assuage their feelings of alienation from their surroundings, families, and friends and to bring meaning to their lives. Through their negotiations of texts from their everyday lives, some struggle against the isolation of individualism and materialism in order to forge bonds with other characters around values of honesty, caring, and freedom. Within this exploration of their identities, they find human connections and they see how the social structure—employment, ownership, and traditional gender relationships—affect their lives. At the end of the film, it is only when they act upon—or write—this new knowledge that they begin to see the possibilities for better, more fulfilling lives. I adapted the film's title for this book in the hope that I might borrow some of its reflective spirit.

Throughout this book, I work with stories taken from my everyday experience as student, teacher, and parent. Although I hope and believe that my stories have some general applications, I start locally, concretely, and personally in order to ground my position in practice and to locate myself within the din of researchers', pundits', and theorists' calls for educational reform. My closeness to my data is a limitation of my work, I'm sure, but it does provide an example of how educators and parents, and perhaps even students can examine the signs and symbols of the events and texts that they encounter. I select stories of adults and children to demonstrate that age is not a concern in developing powers of personal and social reflection. My stories—all stories—do not speak for themselves. Rather, they must be analyzed in order to bring meaning to them within our lives and our social relationships. While I recognize that other plausible analyses can be made of my stories, I attempt to connect those alternatives to different sets of hopes and dreams about how we wish to live together than the ones I hold for my family, children, and society. Currently, the debate about schooling seems mired in concerns about individuals scoring high on local, state, and national tests as preludes to entering the workforce fully prepared. I hope my stories about leadership, control of learning, civic life, and literacy will refocus this debate in order that it will begin to center our concerns of how we help create identities that will enable citizens to read the possibilities and constraints of our social structure and to write a present and future that will be more inclusive, more caring, and more just than our past. Of course, we must teach people to read and write written texts in ways that they will find useful. But we must do much more than that if we are to help them prepare themselves to be powerful negotiators of the meaning of all the texts that influence our lives substantially. For too long, the stories about literacy education have been limited to matters of technique and economics to the detriment of our social condition. I have tried to make *text, lies, & videotape* look beneath and beyond those matters to see where we've been and to point out directions we must go.

Chapter 1

Preparing to Teach and Lead

On most days during a week, I work with teachers or undergraduates. The teachers drive from their schools to take university classes at night or less often during the summer in order to better understand literacy, children, and schooling. The undergraduate "wanna-be" teachers walk to classes and drop by to talk about books, assignments, and registration for classes for the next semester. Both groups remind me of myself at different stages of my schooling. I remember the hour drive one way after teaching all day to take classes three nights a week. I guess I had more energy then because I don't remember feeling exhausted like I do now. I was learning and it seemed worth the time and effort. At least in retrospect it does.

Each year I face several hundred undergraduate students who look and act a lot like I did when I was in school. I don't mean that they are covered with lots of flannel or hair or that they are beer soaked. Rather, they are eager, very white, and a little in awe of university life. They want to be teachers—many want that so badly that they can almost taste the chalk dust, hear the lunch money, and feel the warmth of thirty students in a too-small classroom. Most are earnest and willing to consider any topic that can be related to teaching, children, or schooling. They even endure the din of professors' voices telling them endlessly without the slightest hint of hypocrisy not to lecture. At times, they seem to stare back at me like deer into oncoming headlights.

Those eyes during the day and the teachers' eyes at night ask me to do the impossible—to make them teachers, to make them understand children, and to make them integrate themselves into the community of teachers. For example, at the end of every first class in undergraduate or graduate courses, I ask everyone to write about their reasons for enrolling in the class and their expectations for what they hope to learn during the next fifteen weeks. This begins our negotiations for the direction of our work together.

> I'm in this class as a scout for the other teachers at my school. They want to know if you have anything to offer us. I'm first because I want to try new things to break out of my rut. Your syllabus scares me a little bit. I don't read that much while I'm teaching. In the summer maybe, but not during the school year. I hope those books have lots of ideas that I can use in my classroom. If they don't I probably won't finish the course.
>
> *—teacher enrolled in the Reading/Writing Classroom course*

> This course is required. That's why I'm here. I have a few expectations. The course has a reputation for expecting too much reading. I hope I can keep up. I want to know what to do in 495 [a school-based practicum that follows the reading course]. How do I teach reading? How do I handle the students and the materials? How do I keep my co-op [classroom teacher] and supervisor [university graduate assistant] happy at the same time?
>
> *—undergraduate, enrolled in Teaching Reading*
> *in the Elementary School course*

These and the rest of the undergraduates and teachers expect me to share *the* secret that will do all this for them. This is a terrifying request. At best, I hope to help them prepare themselves to teach, to understand, to integrate. I tell them this, and I am certain that I demonstrate that I do not possess the secret they seek. This is not a dereliction of duty on my part. It is not incompetence. No one can honestly answer their requests. These undergraduates and teachers must construct themselves as teachers through their consideration of their

2

histories, their literacies, and their experiences. That is, they must create their own teacher identities.

I am not without influence, however. After all, I am a text they read during class; I dredge up their histories in new ways; and I sponsor experiences in which they can engage. I am only one among many factors, however, and a fairly minor one at that when compared to the other texts of their lives. My challenge, then, is to attempt to mean something in the lives of those undergraduates and teachers in order that my concerns might affect their identities and those identities that they will influence when they teach. I realize that this sounds arrogant on my part. However, it is the arrogance that all educators must have. We all think that we have something to offer our students, and we all intend to change their lives in both subtle and profound ways. I hope to help them become critically literate so that they can read the explicit and implicit competitions in the texts of their lives in and out of school, analyze the consequences of those competitions for their own and the lives of others, and write more equal and just texts for our future through their teaching and other social engagements.

Like many of the undergraduates and teachers I face, I was the first in either of my parents' families to graduate from college. I too was job oriented and practical by necessity, and I came from a fairly limited background. Because of these shared factors, I listen with knowing ears when undergraduates and teachers talk about schooling and its possibilities. Most of the undergraduates believe that they will return to their hometowns, or at least nearby towns, in order to teach in schools much like the ones they attended. There, they expect that they will fit into the school environment and continue to teach as they were taught. This is not only true of the students I now teach in Pennsylvania, but it is also true of those in Ontario, New York, Minnesota, Indiana, and Texas where I have taught previously.

Moreover, the undergraduates believe that their students will look, talk, and behave as they remember they did when they were younger. Being job oriented, they expect college professors to teach them what to do on a daily basis to make their classroom lives orderly, routine, and enjoyable—all the qualities they perceived in the lives of the teachers who taught them. From personal experience, I know that these predictions and hopes will not always match the realities of their future teaching lives.

I discovered this when I began as a kindergarten teacher in Rochester, New York. Although most of the teachers were first-generation college graduates themselves, I found that few of them believed that their students were college material or likely to be successful in other endeavors. Although we all worked hard at our jobs, we seemed to be losing the struggle to help our students learn much of the school curriculum. Although I grew up in upstate New York, few of the children in my class looked, talked, or acted like me. Not only did they appear different from me, they seemed different from each other. We had boys and girls, of course, who ranged from destitute, poor, and working class to lower middle class. There were also African Americans, Vietnamese, Europeans, European Americans, Haitians, Australians, Asian Americans, and Puerto Ricans, as well as Muslims, Catholics, Jews, non-believers, and a variety of Protestants. Some children were smarter, others were faster, and still others had braces on their legs or thick glasses on their faces. They spoke various dialects of English, French, Greek, Vietnamese, and Spanish. All of them had different backgrounds—some had been to preschool, others had been in foster care; some were immigrants, others were refugees. Two years was the longest anyone had lived at his current address. One had shot his mother accidentally, several were responsible for younger children after school, at least two had been molested, and none was a monolingual small town white male who was making a middle-class wage for the first time, had serious doubts about religion, and had never flown in a plane, ridden in a train, or sailed on a ship.

When I tell this story, the variety of humanity startles many of my undergraduates who seldom think of elementary school students, let alone kindergartners, as real people with real lives. The teachers either roll their eyes in disbelief or nod in agreement. As we talk about the variety among the people in their own communities and classrooms, we invariably begin to explore our views on difference, representation, and multiculturalism as well as less polite ideas about deviance, defiance, and maladjustment. At times, undergraduates and teachers are openly hostile toward difference because the social competitions of our lives force them to see "the other" as wanting to take what they have away from them. More often, however, they see these discussions as irrelevant to their teaching and lives because they work (or will work) in rural, suburban, or small-town school districts that are isolated and safe from "the crises" of multicultural metropolitan areas.

> I would never teach in Philadelphia. There's too much violence. I don't even go to Philadelphia any more like my family did when I was young. There's no need with all the discount malls on the way there. It's dirty and the neighborhoods are dangerous. Everyone has a "club" to keep their car from being stolen. It's not like that where I teach . . . it's peaceful. Everyone's pretty much the same. We have farm kids, but nothing like they do in Philadelphia or even Reading. . . . My students don't really like the multicultural children's books, so I don't use very many.
>
> —*teacher enrolled in the Issues in Literacy Education course*

Although some undergraduates and teachers understand difference as a threat, the majority, while perhaps sympathetic, consider it to be beside the point—something affixed but not central to their development as teachers or even as citizens. They view discussions of difference and multiculturalism as a new imposition upon themselves and their students because they believe that they stand apart from culture and lead "normal" lives. These two beliefs become barriers that keep in place the learning competitions in schools and social competitions outside of schools—competitions that make losers of us all in one way or another. If we hope to eliminate social and learning competitions or at least assuage the savage inequalities that have marred and still mar so much of our lives in and out of schools, we must all analyze these beliefs, where they come from, and who they serve. Moreover, we must recognize ourselves in the oppression of others. This is not self-loathing; rather, it is a reminder of our location in the constellation of privileges and pain that divide our classrooms, schools, communities, nation, and world. It begins our efforts to construct our teaching identities consciously. Without such interrogations of our beliefs and our lives, there is little hope that we can lead our students toward critical literacy and active participation in civic life.

How is it possible for undergraduates, teachers, and most Americans to think that difference and multiculturalism are new issues in the United States? Television, newspapers, and weekly news magazines suggest that the recent influx of immigrants, population growth among preexisting minorities in cities, and the globalization of the economy require teachers and students (in preparation for citizenship) to consider the multicultural composition of our society and world. The fact is, however, that our society has always been multicultural. Well before and well after the European "discovery" of America, this hemisphere's societies were diverse. We have simply ignored or, worse, denied that diversity. School curricula and organization have perpetuated a self-serving or enforced dismissal of this diversity and multiculturalism. This is most clear in the western European male focus of the "great books curriculum" that every American "needs" to know. Too often, current school curricula advocate a cultural tourism in which teachers and students sample the holidays, foods, and arts of other cultures, ethnic groups, and countries—but America is almost never studied in this way. In the margins of these curricula are hidden the many cultures on which wealthy Europeans and now wealthy European Americans have tried to live their normal lives free from culture.

6

When undergraduates or teachers read newspapers and news magazines, remember their Eurocentric great-man history lessons, recall their literature or social studies textbooks, or watch network television or Hollywood films, they find support for their beliefs that they are culture-free and normal and "the other," anyone not apparently just like them, is culture laden and abnormal. Given their school background and this relentless message from popular media, it should be a small wonder that largely white and middle class undergraduates and teachers see multiculturalism as an imposition. One starting point for preparing to lead students toward critical literacy and participation in civic life is factual investigations of the social and cultural differences in United States history and current affairs. Most adults overlook these matters, perhaps in the mistaken belief that the revelation of the contradictions within the American dream would ruin our society.

However, there is more at work here than simple misinformation. Our fears of difference, denial of culture, and claims to be the norm are both mistaken and damaging to ourselves and others. Fear of difference, I think, leads to the systematic weighting of institutional policies and procedures in favor of those in power. Denial of culture precludes our coming to understand ourselves and our relationships to others fully. Claiming to be the norm misrepresents our complexities and the social connections that could lead us to greater control over our lives through individual and collective action in society. To become critically literate, we must explore these convictions to determine what they mean in our lives—what opportunities and constraints they place on us—and what their consequences are for us personally and socially. Moreover, we must place these explorations in the construction of our teaching identities within the context of our search for answers to complicated questions: How do we wish to live together? Do we seek to control others or to achieve equality, privilege or equity, and discrimination or justice for all?

By acknowledging that our personal and collective interests can only be understood in this context, we take a step toward

7

negotiating our existence with people who appear different or atypical to us. To begin those negotiations, we must question our definitions of ourselves as normal and see that such categories are more statements of power than of biological, historical, or even moral fact. For example, when I ask undergraduates and teachers to fill in default values for what it means to be a normal American, they provide answers that sometimes even surprise themselves. Although there is modest disagreement (due to regional, ethnic, and religious pride), they describe a youthful (but not young) white male Protestant who is able bodied (thin and athletic) and able minded (a school graduate), heterosexual, and well off (but not rich). He comes from a two-parent family and from the Northeast. When we quibble about the normal American's ethnic descent, I ask them to name royalty from England, Thailand, or the Netherlands. They know Queen Elizabeth, her mother, Diana and Charles, Charles's brother and sister, Fergie, and the Queen's grandchildren, but no one from the other countries (although some can sing at least part of *The King and I*). We agree that "we" are Anglo-Saxons by media default and, after this exercise, we seldom argue about our definition. When asked to compare this normal American with their reference to themselves as normal (the point from which they judge the difference of the other), we have some surprised looks, some laughs, and some anger. When we consider who benefits from this default definition of American normality that is in most, if not all, of our heads, they stare at me without a twinkle in their eyes.

Since most of the undergraduates and teachers are not normal according to this default definition—in fact, during the last class we had no completely normal Americans enrolled—we begin to investigate why we have this default definition in our heads and how it affects our daily lives. This project involves a critical reading of our pasts, the media, and social customs. For instance, I have students watch the news on television for consecutive nights in order to explore how the media shapes our view of ourselves and others.

I watched Channel 10 for three nights. I was surprised to see who they think is newsworthy. There were women on the screen, but none of them was asked any real questions. When they [the newscasters] offered authoritative sources it was always an old white male. Not just once or twice, but every time. I noticed this first when the news was about economics. Apparently women aren't good with money was the message. Race minorities were treated as criminals or oddballs. They did two stories about murders and one robbery—all the suspects were black men. They did a story about a farmer who carved elaborate lawn ornaments that suburban folks are buying as a joke for their lawns. Message seems to be that farmers (the poor?) are odd. The national news was mostly about wars. Muslims, Somali and Colombian warlords, and North Koreans were the bad guys. Americans, and people who look like us, were the good.

This was an eye-opener for me. I never watched or thought about anything this way before. I don't like it though because it makes me wonder what the real news of the day is. I've got better things to do with my time than to worry about this stuff. I know it's good for me, but so is cauliflower. I don't like that either.

—undergraduate enrolled in a human diversity course

Through these and other activities, we address each marker within the definition in some detail. *White, male,* and *Protestant* are the easiest for us to attribute to schooling, government, and daily life. From a linguistic analysis of the phrase *man and wife* in some marriage ceremonies to demographic analyses of Congress and census data, undergraduates and teachers quickly see how those markers are reinforced. *Youthful* and *able bodied* require critical reading of the mail we receive, commercials, and what we watch on television and at the movies. The images presented in these advertisements affect our beliefs about ourselves and others and create desires that through repetition become our beliefs. Once we begin to read these texts in new ways, we can't stop finding additional examples for how the default definition is perpetuated. It seems impossible now to avoid them in the clothing catalogs, television diet ads, and billboards that invade our mailboxes, homes, and communities.

"Family values"—*male dominated, heterosexual,* and *two parents*—seem to come from home and church. But we find reinforcers everywhere. Single parents are practically charged with child neglect in news magazines, through government reports, on television, and in movies. Disney's favorite theme seems to be the two-parent, heterosexual family even when the film appears to be about singles and sex (for example, *Pretty Woman,* 1990, Touchstone). Discussion of these markers causes some distress among us because family values seem to cut across religious lines in ways that the other markers do not. While some accept all markers as socially determined, others through their faith are unwilling or unable to accept that these family values were not written in stone.

Being *well-off* is also a ticklish point to discuss in class because we are conflicted about our economic status. We seem to wish we were better off, but we also believe that we are about as well off as everyone else. We laugh when George Bush wore a flannel shirt or a hard hat or Bill Clinton ate at McDonald's during the 1992 presidential campaign because we know that Bush, Clinton, and others of their economic class are not like us. But at the same time we see on television and in newspaper ads and catalogs and magazines that we should have bigger houses, faster cars, and more things than we are able to purchase. That is, we want to be more like the Bushes and Clintons of the world, but overall, we see America as a middle-class country with a graduated tax system that helps us maintain our economic position. As we begin to read other symbols and documents, however, we learn that our view has been obscured.

Juxtaposing a Pulitzer Prize–exposé on economics in the *Philadelphia Inquirer* (later to be published as *America: What Went Wrong?* by Ronald L. Barlett and James B. Steele 1992, Andrews and McMeel), the 1992 presidential campaign literature from both Republicans and Democrats, and the front and economic pages of our local papers, undergraduates and teachers read that we are rapidly approaching a two-class society within the United States—the rich and the rest. We can still divide annual salary and wages into three categories: the poor (39 percent of all 1990 tax filers earned below fifteen thousand dollars), the middle class (57 percent earned between fifteen and seventy-five thousand dollars) and the rich (4 percent filed above seventy-five thousand dollars). However, these economic categories no longer explain very much because the rich now receive as much in salary and wages as the bottom 50 percent of the taxpayers (all the poor and half of the middle class). By contrast, in 1959 the top 4 percent of filers made as much through salary and wages as the bottom 35 percent. And the gap is widening at an accelerated rate. During the 1980s, incomes of the rich increased between 69 and 218 percent *annually*, depending on whether their salaries were closer to seventy-five-thousand or the one-million-dollar mark. On the other hand, the total income of middle-class filers only increased an average 4 percent each year and the income of the poor actually declined.

This redistribution of wealth didn't just happen by accident. The unequal consequences from the competition for income in the United States is the explicit result of governmental policy. For example, 1986 tax reform legislation was supposed to equalize the tax burden across classes and ensure that everyone would pay some taxes. In fact, it was a windfall for the rich, who received two or three times the percentage tax cut as the poor or the middle class. While the average teacher with a salary in the mid-thirty-thousand-dollar range received an 11 percent tax cut and put approximately 467 more dollars annually in a bank account, CEOs with average salaries in the 750,000-dollar range received a 34 percent tax cut that put approximately eighty-six thousand more dollars at their disposal. Those making over a million dollars a year received a 31 percent cut, leaving them with an additional 280,000 dollars in after-tax income. At best, the poor received a 9 percent tax reduction and pocketed an extra 50 bucks.

The fact that supposedly neutral institutions skew social competitions systematically toward society's powerful is news to most teachers and undergraduates. It makes them angry and reflective at the same time. They begin to question how other "neutral" institutions sponsor unequal competitions and use normality to hide bias. For many of us, it is the first time that we have considered the possibility that our language, thoughts, and categories are not scientific certainties but socially determined and how social institutions can work against "abnormal" Americans'—that is, our—best interests. Moreover, the fact that we might be directly or indirectly implicated in these inequalities is difficult for us to consider, but it is impossible for us to deny. When our thoughts turn to schooling and our roles in education, the assumptions and structure of psychological and cultural literacy perspectives, which suggest that difference is deficit or depravity, curricula built of skills or the best of the past are natural, and learning requires competitions, seem arbitrary and self-serving for those who have wealth, position, and power.

> All this talk about liberty and justice for all is just that, talk. The tax system works for the rich. That should be expected when all of Congress is rich. The government can be bought, health care can be bought, and the legal system can be bought. Where does that leave me? I have no money. All my salary covers is my expenses of raising two kids. . . . I've always thought of myself as middle class and "normal," but now I see that those labels don't really mean anything. It's money that matters. Those labels make me feel superior and safe (at least I'm not unemployed, poor, or weird). But like you said in your last letter, you can't eat feelings of superiority or comfort. I want justice—economic justice—for me and for everyone because except for the wealthy we're in this together, only we just don't know it. I mean the labels keep us apart. Those labels come from school, the media, and I hate to admit it, from church.
> *—letter from a teacher*

These critical readings of institutional, social, and commercial texts demystify the concept of normality and reveal the politics of media, schooling, and everyday life. No longer are the markers of the default definition of normality in America separated from culture and beyond analysis. Being white, male, or Protestant does not naturally connote privilege, moral superiority, or power. Of course, neither do any other social markers. We are all cultural and social beings who are shaped and are shaping history. We learn that history (human action) rather than fate or nature is what drives our social interactions, identities, and institutions, and that we can influence our lives—control them to a greater extent—if we can find ways to deal with our differences without fear or jealousy. That is, we believe that we can find more just and equitable ways to live together.

Within the question of finding ways to live together, our exploration of our positions on difference requires us to consider our stances on the possibilities of just and harmonious living among the diversity of our classrooms and communities. Most undergraduates and teachers believe that educators must be tolerant of difference if harmony is the goal. "If all of us could just learn to tolerate each other, then things would be fine," they say in various ways. However, on critical reflection, we recognize that tolerance is not sufficient to address this issue because it implies continued unequal power relationships. Tolerance means literally overcoming one's own resistance to that which is distasteful or antagonistic. While I, as the epitome of the normal American (OK, so I'm not that fit or youthful) can be graciously tolerant of women, people of color, gays and lesbians, the disabled, the old or young, people who speak languages or dialects other than my own, believers, the poor or wealthy, orphans or single parents and their children, or non–New Englanders (all of whom I might find distasteful), they must live by rules in schools and laws and social mores in society that have often been arranged to benefit me—that is, the normal American. The Other cannot be tolerant; rather the Other must submit to (or resist as "outlaws") "my" system because they do not have the power of equal choice. There is no justice in tolerance. We must do better than tolerance in our search to find ways to live together because tolerance can only mask oppression.

Moreover, reducing our interest in just and harmonious living within a diverse society to issues of tolerance, we again lose sight of the hidden similarities in our relative economic positions. My students and I need the Other and they need us if we are to struggle for social, political, and economic justice and harmony. In this instance, personal and social interests coincide. Rather than tolerance, what we must find are ways that enable us to join together in those struggles while we locate, celebrate, and interrogate our differences.

In order to work toward fair and equitable relationships, we must affirm individuals' and social groups' right to be and remain different from one another without an assumption of hierarchies. That is, we must expose and oppose the concept of normality encoded in "rules, laws, and scores" as the frame of reference from which to judge the value of human beings or their cultures. We must dismantle the rigged competitions we use to mystify our social constructions of inequality and injustice. And we must stop fooling ourselves that Americans can share the same set of characteristics and values without doing violence to the lives and cultures of most people who inhabit America. We must acknowledge our differences and work toward collective explanations of how people differ, where those differences come from, and how we can live and work together *with* (not despite) those differences.

By recognizing that our predictions about schooling and our teaching might not be accurate, by locating ourselves within America's diversity, and by acknowledging that the social practices of school and society that we have taken for granted have made us and our institutions cruel, my students and I expand our sense of what it means to be practical and job oriented in our study of teaching, children, and our professional relationships. Of course, we must study curricular and instructional practices that seem to direct teachers' efforts on a daily basis, but we now recognize that these practices are not benign, neutral, or nonpolitical. Rather, we study them within the context of our understanding of the unequal human relationships within America and our hopes about how we wish to live together. We now see that curricular content, instructional strategies, and evaluative focus are ways—perhaps teachers' primary ways—to express our particular visions of what knowledge is of most worth, what it means to know something, and how we might understand ourselves, others, and the world.

From our critical reading of the competitive, biased arrangements of most current school practices, frameworks, and policies, we learn that schools in general and literacy programs in particular are often organized to promote a specific set of values—normal American values.

> After you look at basals [systems of textbooks for teaching reading] and how they are used in elementary school reading programs, it's easy to see why the town kids in Heath's study did better than the black or white working class kids. [Shirley Brice Heath is an anthropologist from Stanford who studied three sections of a school district just after school desegregation laws began to be enforced in the Carolina Piedmont.] The content, the language, the directions are all set to match what the children from the town brought with them to school. The teachers think that it's the kids' natural ability that shines through. But Heath's teachers showed that all the kids had the ability to learn well if they were treated appropriately. Before she [Heath] arrived the traditional programs not only discriminated against blacks, but the poor, ESL [English as a Second Language], and maybe even girls. The schools wanted to blame the homes and cultures of these kids, but Heath showed them that their (our) system was (is) biased.
>
> *—teacher enrolled in the Issues in Education course*

To this point during the semester, we have developed a fairly sophisticated language of critique for our teaching identities, but we have yet to specify how this critique will effect our teaching lives and our social actions. Here we often split company. A significant portion of undergraduates and teachers believe schooling toward normal American values is "a good thing" because it gives everyone an opportunity to succeed upon graduation. They assume that if "different" individuals can assume normal values and skills they will be rewarded by society. To arrange schooling to explore diversity, they argue, handicaps "abnormal" Americans and ensures their second-class citizenship.

> Delpit is right. [Lisa Delpit, an anthropologist at Morgan State University in Baltimore makes a theoretical argument that certain learner-centered approaches to English education work against African American students' best interests.] It's a biased system and if you don't learn the power codes you have no chance for success in this country. That is what we've learned since the beginning of this course. Schools should teach the power language [Standard English] and the power content [the literacy canon and American and European history] to the have-nots in society so that they can compete. Without this information they'll be lucky to work at McDonald's and certainly not The Gap. That's our job, to give them the skills, the values, the power codes. Anything else is racism.
>
> —*undergraduate enrolled in the Teaching Reading in the Elementary School course*

However, others object to this biased organization of schooling as unfair, and they point to similar injustices outside of schooling in housing, employment, and health care. They argue that even skilled women hit their heads on glass ceilings at work, that even affluent people of color are redlined from living in certain neighborhoods, and many employed individuals and their families are without proper health care. For them, acquisition of normal American values and traditional school skills and content are not tickets to ride in the economic or social fast lane because the biases that separate different life-paths continue to operate regardless of an individual's knowledge of "power codes." Their objections range from modest concerns for adjustments of those institutions and systems in order to bring about more equal opportunity to complete rejections of traditional school and social organizations and practices to bring about equity of outcome.

The system sucks. I know that's not professional, but it does suck. I don't see how you can do good by doing bad. If I know that concepts of "normal" or "grade level" or "learning disabled" really hide the unfairness of the system, how can the power code, which is built to protect that system, help minorities? I mean, if the power code means power, then why would the powerful let others learn it? My grandfather didn't graduate from grade school and he became a state trooper. My father had to go to junior college to get a good job. I'll be lucky to find a job with a college diploma. The stick gets higher for the next generation. Learning the power code would help minorities only if the system wasn't biased. But. . . . We have to do something about the system.

*—undergraduate enrolled in the Teaching Reading in
the Elementary School course*

This second group speaks with a language of hope in search of ways to engender the exploration of diversity at school on a daily, even hourly basis. They recognize that learning skills and content—the power code—is not necessarily separate from thoughtful considerations of difference and its social consequences. Moreover, they believe that thoughtful consideration must lead to deliberate action. Those undergraduates and teachers want to learn what we can *do* about the injustices we have experienced and identified. This concern for action moves us forward in two ways.

First, we must develop or learn about alternative and more fair school programs and classroom structures. How can schools be organized so that they do not divide students along differences in order to conquer? How can teachers know and use the literacies that students bring to school in order to help them understand themselves, each other, and the social systems? And how can we stop all the biased competition in the daily activities of the classroom? Fortunately, these undergraduates and teachers don't have to start from scratch because like-minded educators have over a century of practice and theories to influence our thoughts about equitable

17

schooling from preschool to postsecondary education. These examples help undergraduates and teachers to prepare to act differently when teaching—leading them to seek multiaged classes, to fight against reified curricular goals in rigid sequences, to group cooperatively by interest, to struggle against the biased competition among social groups disguised as ability grouping, and to negotiate rules for learners in order to establish learning communities to increase our students' stake in classroom and school life.

Second, we address the paralyzing attitude reflected in sayings like "You can't fight city hall." Analyses of the structure of schooling and society can leave educators with the feeling that they are pawns in someone else's game of chess. They begin to doubt their abilities to act independently of the "invisible hand" that seems to direct us all. Although they see and abhor the biases, they doubt their abilities to make much of a difference in "the system." This doubt is exacerbated by undergraduates' initial trips to area schools and teachers' observations of their own workplace because neither group finds many examples of learner-centered education in practice and virtually no examples of students engaging actively in civic life. Although they find some classrooms where difference is being explored thoughtfully, they find many teachers practicing isolated skills and "normal" facts very much in evidence with all the biases we have identified in our investigations. When they are bold enough to inquire as to the rationale for organizing lessons as learning competitions, they are told in various ways that "That's how all children are taught. This is the real world, not the university classroom."

If left unchallenged, this doubt begins to erode many undergraduates' and teachers' interest in "doing things differently," and they shy away from the struggle toward creating alternative pedagogy altogether. Accordingly, we confront these feelings directly and ground our consideration in undergraduates' and teachers' own lives. To begin, we write autobiographic descriptions of what we remember about learning to read and write at home and at school. We talk with our parents and grandparents, look at the artifacts our elders have saved, and reflect upon our days as students within reading and language arts lessons. We share these personal histories in class in order to see commonalities and differences across classmates. We learn that parts of our histories are not personal at all but are shared by many. Other parts are unique.

> Everyone in our group used an SRA [Scientific Research Associates] kit in fourth grade. Can you believe it? Five people from all over Pennsylvania, New York, and New Jersey and we used the same box of cards with texts on the front and questions on the back? I hated that box. I never got beyond orange—Tiffany says she finished the whole box that year. I doubt it. I can remember my teacher ragging on me to finish the orange like the rest of the group. I hated those things and I still hate the color orange and think I'm a bad reader even though I'm in the honors program.
>
> *—undergraduate student in the Teaching Reading in the Elementary School course*

> I learned to read on my grandmother's lap. She'd read it, then I'd read it. She smelled of bread—she made the best bread I ever tasted. She put jam on it if she thought I did a good job. And she always did. That's how I learned. At school we sang the alphabet song and read Dick and Jane. We wrote letters. That's the only writing I can remember. But I learned to read by sitting with my grandmother, then next to her when I grew too big. She told me I was smart and pretty when I know I was neither. She was a wonderful woman and I miss her.
>
> *—teacher enrolled in the Reading/Writing Classroom course*

Through sharing and interrogating our memories, we begin to question how the official histories of learning traditionally projected by methods textbooks, teacher colleges, and schools could be so different than the collective history we construct in class. To help us to situate our class work in a larger historical and theoretical context, we read and discuss my books *The Struggle to Continue* (1990) and *Becoming Political* (1992). The first book discusses the human intentions behind traditional practices and introduces educators who tried to eliminate learning competitions, to explore difference, and to employ other perspectives over the last one hundred years. The second places those acts in a theoretical framework to offer intellectual depth to our construction of teaching identities and provides seven "projects of possibility" in which administrators, classroom teachers, and special education teachers acted on their emerging critical teaching identities within their own classrooms, schools, or school districts.

Our work together offers us the opportunity to gaze at the similarity and diversity in an apparently homogeneous setting much like my hometown. One of our goals is to see diversity among groups that appear similar and the similarity among apparently diverse groups. A second goal is to question our belief that teaching is knowing all the answers or finding ways to manage students in order to make it through the school day, week, and year. With these questions, we learn to lead students to critique the values and behaviors which the media and other institutions attempt to impose on them and to develop their own identities. By learning about ourselves; our connections with culture and difference; the social construction of language, norms, and institutions; and some historical and current alternatives to school and social biases, we begin to remake ourselves as teachers, leaders, and historical beings who can make changes through our actions. One place to start is by taking ownership of our learning.

> I have spent the last three weeks intently analyzing countless issues that class discussions and readings have brought to me. We did research and worked in groups, but the most I learned came from my own thoughts outside of class, thinking about and applying the issues. . . . I have also seen many people growing and struggling as I am. Hearing the testimonies of others has given me a bit of confidence to work through the roadblocks. . . . I do not want to sit on the fence about all these issues, like I do now. I want to firmly plant my feet on the ground and defend my position. This class has given me the foundation and desire to do so. I don't want to just take classes anymore; I want an education.
>
> —*teacher enrolled in the Reading/Writing Classroom course*

Chapter 2

Seeing the Importance and Limits of Ownership in Learning

*O*ur daughter, Laura, attends the Friends School of State College. Four years ago, when Laura was six years old and in first grade, her mother (Kathleen), her three-year-old brother (Tim-Pat), and I taught in Laura's classroom once a week, supporting students' writing, reading, and mathematics. Laura's teacher, Teacher Eileen (TE), allowed us time and choice to pursue our own projects while teaching. Kathleen literally built the school library (the collection, the card catalog, and even the shelves); she conferred with students about their writing; and she started a K–1 newspaper. I shared books with students, listened to them read, and taught some mathematics. Tim-Pat enjoyed the listening center and the blocks.

Reading and writing instruction is directed at individuals at Friends School. From the first day, students are expected to write and read, and they are given time to do both. During that time, students select books arranged in dish tubs to read according to their interests and abilities. These texts range from wordless picture books to chapter books in order to accommodate the differing interests and abilities in the classroom. Once books are selected, students find places they wish to read. Some select rocking chairs, others tables, and still others curl up on the rugs near the bookshelves. All are expected to read for at least twenty minutes, while the teacher circulates to listen to students and to discuss their selection and understanding of those books. When they finish a book, students are invited to share it—read and talk about it—with their classmates. This individualized reading program takes place in a classroom that drips with print and that requires students to read labels, signs, and messages from teachers and other students. It works quite well—Laura and her classmates read often and eagerly.

When writing, students select topics, genre, and style in order to write what they mean and to give expression to their experiences. They write for their peers, and their completed work varies from posters to patterned language books to collected reports to chapter stories. Laura was expected to write a draft, to confer with classmates and adults while composing in order to help with the sense of the piece, to meet with an adult to edit the finished draft, to make changes accordingly, to send the edited copy to a typist, to illustrate the text, and then to present the finished book to the class. All student books become the property of the classroom library and were placed in the book tubs.

Rarely did I visit the classroom without someone asking me to read his or her book. All seemed eager to write their stories. Although the organization of the literacy program was very different than the one I experienced as a student—students reading in all positions from different books and writing texts of their own at rates that boggled my mind—there was organization. Students recognized that their freedom to choose what to read and write also brought the responsibility to read and write, to discuss and present, and to begin anew and continue. Of course, there was more noise and movement than in traditional classrooms, but there is also more reading and writing taking place. In many traditional elementary school classrooms, students read connected text (such as stories or articles) less than six minutes a day, and they write such texts once or twice a month. In Laura's classroom, both averages were often exceeded daily before the literacy period was a third completed.

This organization, these rules, and these routines were not posted on the walls or repeated endlessly by teachers. Rather, because they had kindergartners and first graders together, the older students—the veterans—taught the younger ones the ropes. This too is a sight to behold—six year olds demonstrating how to select, read, and present a book and how to draft, edit, and share their writings. It didn't work perfectly each day, but nine days out of ten each student read a book of her or his choice for at least twenty minutes and wrote for over thirty minutes. Fortunately, that tenth day was staggered among members of the class so that there was never a total breakdown. In a sense, the students owned the literacy education program with all the rights and responsibilities of ownership.

According to many experts—teacher educators, sociolinguists, and teachers—ownership is considered the cornerstone of literacy education.

> With the best topic, the child exercises strongest control, establishes ownership and with ownership, pride in the piece he or she is writing. (Donald Graves, *Writing: Teachers and Children at Work*, 1984, Heinemann)

> What should never be forgotten, however, is that the *force* of revision in writing, the energy of ownership, is rooted in the child's voice, the urge to express. (Donald Graves, *Writing: Teachers and Children at Work*, 1984, Heinemann)

> If we want our adolescent students to grow to appreciate literature, another first step is allowing them to exert ownership and choose the literature they will read. (Nancy Atwell, *In the Middle: Writing, Reading, and Learning with Adolescents*, 1987, Boynton/Cook)

> Authenticity is essential. Kids need to feel that what they are doing through language, they have chosen to do because it is useful or interesting or fun for them. They need to own the processes they use: to feel that the activities are their own; not just school work or stuff to please the teacher. What they do ought to matter to them personally. (Kenneth Goodman, *What's Whole in Whole Language?*, 1986, Scholastic)

By having ownership in what they do, by following their own questions about topics, they are able to create new concepts and make new connections in their schemata. They select and take on projects; they make them their own, thereby making their knowledge their own. It is this ownership that fosters intellectual autonomy. "Owning" an activity or project leads to knowing how, why and what to do. (Christine Pappas, Barbara Kiefer, and Linda Levstik, *An Integrated Language Perspective in the Elementary School*, 1990, Longman)

To own a topic, a book, an activity, or a process appears to be fundamental to learning to use language purposefully to pursue one's interests. For most of us, ownership is what separates our consuming interest in hobbies and our compelling interest in our jobs—so many of us do not own our work and find less control, voice, choice, authenticity, and intellectual autonomy in our vocations than we do when pursuing our avocations. Teachers should acknowledge this fact and develop conditions that will not only permit but will facilitate students' ownership of their literacy during and after school. I've seen it work, but ownership is not so straightforward as it first appears.

In a fit of enthusiasm, Kathleen and I proposed to Laura's class that we rewrite some folktales, perform them before video cameras, and sell them as a fundraiser for other class projects. At the very least, we hoped to read many folktales to them, to develop a loose definition of a folktale, to discuss story parts (characters, plots, settings, and so on), to consider how different versions of the same story suggested cross-cultural similarities, to talk about different genres (stories versus plays) and media (book versus film), and to encourage student ownership of their literacy and literacy artifacts. TE, the school administrator, and the parents supported our initiative, and we began by collecting and reading a wide variety of folktales aloud on three successive Tuesdays. We planned on two more weeks to prepare and perform our versions.

Things went well until we finished reading the first book on the first Tuesday. We intended that after each reading we would discuss the tale's plot, compare it to other tales, and begin to induce a definition of folktales to direct our selection and adaptation for our video plays. During the first discussion, students were reluctant to comment on the book other than to compare it to the Disney and *Fairy Tale Theater* (CBS/Fox videos) versions many had seen in theaters or on television. We followed the first folktale with another version of the same tale, but Laura's classmates clung tenaciously to the verity of the film or televised version they had experienced. To them, our two versions of *Snow White* were cute, terrible, or scary depending on the student's personal tastes, but all agreed that when these versions strayed from Disney, they were wrong.

Perhaps Kathleen, TE, and I should have expected this. When we thought about it, we all remembered where and when we first saw *Snow White and the Seven Dwarfs* many years ago. As I write about this incident now "Whistle While You Work" seeps into my thoughts. Why shouldn't a five-year-old ask, "When do they sing 'Whose Afraid of the Big Bad Wolf?'" as we read Paul Galdone's version of *The Three Little Pigs* (1979, Clarion)? All the same, we were startled by the strength of Disney's grip on these children's thoughts about folktales.

Although multiple versions of the same folktale helped a little, we didn't start to make real progress on interpreting folktales until we read Jon Scieszka and Lane Smith's *The True Story of the Three Little Pigs by A. Woolf* (1989, Viking). This book retells the familiar tale from the wolf's point of view—how he was a victim of circumstance and societal prejudice against wolves. The version is unexpected and humorous and the students started giggling almost from the first word. Reading this book aloud both facilitated and constrained our discussions. Students were more willing to talk about and "play" with the ideas of folktales, but thereafter they limited their discussions to the three tales *The Three Little Pigs*, *The Three Bears*, and *The Three Billy Goats Gruff*.

Each group rewrote a folktale—sometimes through pictures, sometimes with teachers acting as scribes, and sometimes with "We'll work it out during the play." Each declared a title and decided who would play which part. These steps overlapped considerably. For example, in one retelling of *The Three Bears*, three students chose to be Goldilocks, and the play was written accordingly. However, when the one Bear disclosed her plans to wear a bear skin during the play, two Goldilocks switched to Bear parts, and the play had to be rewritten.

On the fourth Tuesday, students settled upon four titles and plots: *The Three Billy Goats Gruff* (an exact copy of the traditional tale); *Two Pigs and a Wolf* (a story about a wolf visiting two sleeping pigs); *Goldilocks and Thunderbolt* (a traditional retelling except that Goldilocks rode everywhere on a winged unicorn); and *Goldilocks and the Three Bears: The Day After*.

Goldilocks and the Three Bears: The Day After reversed the plot of the traditional folktale, added a detail from *Cinderella*, and twisted the climax. You see, Goldilocks left her shoes at the Bear's residence when she jumped out the window ("You always take your shoes off when you lie on a bed"), and the Bears, who as Paul Galdone (1985, Clarion) suggests in his version of the tale, "Never did anyone any harm," decided to return them to Goldilocks. Luckily, Goldilocks had attended day care, and, of course, "Her name and address were written inside her shoes." So it was easy for the Bears to find Goldilocks's house. Just before the Bears arrived, Goldilocks had cooked spaghetti and left for a walk while it cooled. Finding the house open, the Bears entered ("Friends open the door and yell 'Anybody home?'"); they ate the spaghetti ("Not to be mean, but it smelled so good"); they sat down to rest in the only chair available ("They were tired after a long walk and a good meal"); broke it; and then they lay on her bed upstairs ("There was no place else to sit").

Upon her return Goldilocks was not pleased to find the spaghetti eaten, her chair broken, and three Bears in her bed. When she demanded an explanation, the Bears replied that they were only trying to return her shoes from the day before. Goldilocks then apologized for "messing up" their

26

house too. The Bears acknowledged that they now "see how easy it is to mess up someone else's house." "You haven't eaten yet" said the Middle-Sized Bear. "Let's go out and have some spaghetti." Goldilocks and the Bears shook hands and went off arm in arm in search of a meal.

Through this story I hope to elaborate upon the opportunities and constraints the theory of ownership places on the understanding of students' language and literacy development. The Friends School literacy program was designed for students to have rights and responsibilities of ownership so that they would tell their stories as they developed individual identities. The folktale project provides an explicit example of how that ownership was negotiated between and among the teachers and students. With ownership would come students' control, voice, choice, authenticity, and intellectual autonomy in order to use literacy for their own purposes. Let me be more explicit.

Although it could be argued that Kathleen and I owned this folktale project (because we initiated it) and TE owned the context in which the project took place (because she allowed all of us to begin), Friends School students owned the content, structure, characters, and actions of the video plays. The students negotiated among themselves which folktales would be rewritten (we had multiple versions of sixteen available), what the plots would be, how those plots would be enacted, who would play which part, and why the characters would behave and talk in certain ways. This control enabled students to find themselves within the project, and it set the project apart from other activities in which children are expected to fill active roles that adults define for them (for example, the Suzuki method of teaching young children learning to play instruments). That adults were involved in the project did not diminish the students' pride in their work, but it did provide a realistic experience of control.

While discussing books, rewriting folktales, and directing plays, students found opportunities to express themselves creatively and to have their thoughts and actions considered

27

seriously by their peers and teachers. The rewritten folktales and their reiteration in video form became artifacts of students' voices to which students could return in order to examine how these texts represent just who they were at the moment and, perhaps, who they wished to become. The project offered each student an extended opportunity to experiment in the ongoing process of the development and refinement of a personal voice.

Students chose which folktales they wanted to retell, but they were not free to choose to write a different story. They chose with which group they would work, which part to take within the play, and which props would be necessary. On one occasion, a group chose to start all over again rather than to continue with a script that no longer fit their interests. Jamie chose not to participate in the video plays, but decided she could be involved directly in "rolling the credits" at the beginning of each videotape. Students could exercise the right of choice (not just pick among teacher-offered options) only during those aspects of the project over which they had ownership.

The project had real purpose for the students. They were going to create two texts—one written and one videotaped—in order to raise money for an agricultural project they wished to attempt. In this way the project was authentic, although several of the activities within the project were con- trived by teachers in order to explore what possible texts the students might create. That is, teachers had some authentic academic goals for the project as well.

The videos were the students' creation. They developed or decided to reproduce the stories, characters, and sets for stag- ing. Beyond these artifacts, they made some discoveries that should help them to examine how other stories are told, writ- ten, or performed. In order to prepare to rewrite the stories, students engaged in several levels of analysis of the folktales written by a variety of authors for various reasons. In short, students created new knowledge for themselves and new pro- cesses of critique that may enable them to demonstrate an independence of mind if they continue to develop and practice these skills in other settings. The project was a demonstration of students' intellectual autonomy.

Ownership, then, is a useful concept for coming to understand how children—and all people—learn particular content and processes under particular conditions either individually in reading and writing programs such as the one at the Friends School or through group projects like the folktale unit. Ownership of process and product is clearly linked to control, voice, choice, authenticity, and intellectual autonomy, which are desired outcomes of schooling. In this sense, teachers and students must own their classrooms, their language and learning, and their entire educative experience. So considered, this theory of ownership seems positive, simple, and straightforward. However, it is also limiting, simplistic, and misleading.

Certainly ownership provides opportunities for learners, but the theory that underlies it misrepresents what is really taking place when children are said to own their language, literacy, and learning. This theory causes adults to misread what is happening as they observe children's learning and to miss opportunities to help children come to understand themselves, their histories, and their cultures better. In short, ownership begins the process of people coming to know themselves and to use language and literacy for their own purposes, but because it focuses too narrowly on the individual and the personal, ownership denies them access to analysis of their identities—who they are and what they want to make of themselves.

During our folktale project in Laura's classroom, the importance of this caveat becomes most clear in the climactic twist in *Goldilocks and the Three Bears: The Day After*. Goldilocks and the Bears negotiated a settlement for their disagreement instead of running from their responsibilities as in the traditional versions. They did not fight because of their disagreement as in *The Three Billy Goats Gruff* or *Two Pigs and a Wolf.* Rather, this group of five- and six-year-olds radically departed from the violence of traditional folktales. Why?

Abby, Laura, Walton, and Zahra, the authors and actors of *Goldilocks and the Three Bears: The Day After*, can be distinguished from their classmates primarily by the length of their enrollment in the Friends School. Other groups had similar mixtures of gender, race, age, and ethnic backgrounds, but the majority of the other groups had not attended Friends School for more than two months at the time of the project. Abby, Laura, and Walton had attended Friends School for an entire year and had participated in the explicit and implicit curriculum of nonviolent conflict resolution. Even in this artificial context of the video plays, they invoked a Quaker voice—they found a peaceful solution to their conflict. In this instance, the Quaker Meeting can lay claim to partial ownership of their particular video play in ways that it cannot lay claim to the others.

Similarly, we should not suggest that individual Friends School students owned the choices that they made during the folktale project. Their choices were influenced by the opportunities and constraints that their exposure to popular culture offered them. For example, the Walt Disney Corporation had a pronounced impact on the process of interpreting and choosing folktales. Despite the diversity of backgrounds among this Friends School class, they shared the experience of watching and sometimes reading Disney versions of many folktales—and probably the same folktales many times. Although the medium may be the message as Marshall McLuan once proclaimed, the allure of Disney's movies, television shows, books, and paraphernalia colored their individual interpretations of the world substantially. Without explicit intent, perhaps, the values and implicit social relations of the Disney Corporation are embedded in the ideas, actions, and choices of most North Americans during the latter half of the twentieth century. Given the success of Disney's *The Little Mermaid, Beauty and the Beast, Aladdin,* and *The Lion King,* this influence should continue well into the next century. Does Disney have partial ownership of the folk-tale project and our profits?

Ownership, then, is more complex than the experts lead us to believe. While valuable, it provides the illusion of individualism and masks the origins of values, attitudes, and opinions. If people are to come to understand themselves and others through literacy, then they must push past the illusion of singular personal ownership and voice to acknowledge the social groups who speak through them. In this way, we can locate ourselves and others in the social constellations that surround us. This is not often easy, even when we are equipped with the broadened theory of ownership, as my family experience attests.

Unlike Laura, Tim-Pat did not begin kindergarten with outward demonstrations that he could draw, read, or write. Before beginning school, he rarely picked up a pencil or crayon. Tim-Pat loved to listen and comment on stories; he'd copy thank-you notes from our examples to avoid our threat of making him send back his presents; he enjoyed pretend play, television shows, and movies; but he did not make much use of our chalk board, tablets, crayons, magazines, books, or the computer to draw pictures or write or read on his own. During the summer before he went to kindergarten, we did entice him to dictate his first reports about his sports persona, J.C., who dreams he is the son of Randall Cunningham (the quarterback for the Philadelphia Eagles).

Although Kathleen and I were not openly concerned about his literacy and schooling, I think we were both a little surprised when he came home from his first day of school with a very intricate drawing of some tanks and airplanes in a "fire fight" represented by dashes between the two sets of objects on the sheet. We asked him where he had learned to draw like that, and he told us that he sat down next to some first-grade boys at a classroom table and imitated what they were doing.

We are used to Tim-Pat, the observer. We have watched him construct the rules for how to accomplish something—work the VCR, assemble a toy, or tie his shoes—by simply watching someone else doing it and then experimenting with the behaviors until he can perform the task himself. We were prepared for him to learn the etiquette of the classroom quickly, to pick up procedures, to excel at recess, gym, and music. But we were unprepared for his rapid control of drawing and visual storytelling.

Moreover, we were totally unprepared on the fifth day of school when he wrote and illustrated his first book, *Sharks*. Tim-Pat was particularly pleased that, during his peer editing process, he had surprised his group by not detailing the wonder and horrors of sharks but by listing the different sports that these sharks could play in the Atlantic Ocean. "I can make the shark do whatever I want," he proclaimed—a clear statement of both the power of literacy and of ownership. TE told Kathleen that he had even accepted a peer editor's question by adding another page, "Sharks box," to his ten-page book. We were astonished when he showed us his rough draft, which included appropriate vowel and consonant combinations in his invented spellings. Where had all this come from?

During the next several weeks of kindergarten, Tim-Pat wrote and published *Colonial Times*, *The Civil War in Texas*, *J.C. Plays T-Ball*, *T-Ball*, and *World War 2*. We celebrated the first couple of books with author parties, but after our initial euphoria that we had another writer in the family, Kathleen and I became a little concerned about the pattern we saw developing in Tim-Pat's story lines. We could track the attraction to baseball—we attended several games that year and our family plays baseball in the backyard, but neither of us could figure out where the war themes came from. Granted, Tim-Pat watched *Ninja Turtles*, *Star Wars*, and the like. He loved video games that celebrate the punching and kicking of villains until they disappear. But where had he learned about the American War of Independence (the subject of *Colonial Times*), the Civil War, and World War II? We visited Williamsburg, Virginia, last year, where he stood stunned by the eight hundred musket rifles that line the Governor's Mansion walls and ceilings. Because we live in Pennsylvania, we have driven past but not visited Gettysburg. We couldn't even begin to imagine where he had discovered World War II.

Kathleen and I worried about the propriety of Tim-Pat drawing war pictures and writing war stories at a Friends School founded on the pedagogy of nonviolence. This was not a concern about political correctness. Rather, we wanted Tim-Pat to understand why Friends choose nonviolence and shun wars. At dinner one night, I couldn't stand the ambiguity any longer, and I asked Tim-Pat about his writing, being careful to begin by reaffirming that his mother and I were very proud of him and his literary accomplishments. However, I quickly turned to his interest in writing about war and how that topic squared with the class discussions about nonviolent conflict resolution.

He told me that he wasn't sure why he wrote about wars and rationalized his actions by reporting that other students were writing such stories. Unabated, I told him that I wasn't sure why others might be interested in war, but that I wanted him to know the consequences of war, like dropping bombs and shooting from tanks. At the time, President Clinton was deciding whether to send more troops to North Korea, Somalia, and/or Haiti. We referred to *Hiroshima No Pika* (Maruki, 1982, Lothrup), *Sami and the Time of Troubles* (Heide & Gilliland, 1992, Clarion), and other books that discussed the consequences of war and that we had read to him previously. Tim-Pat sat in silence, absorbing our concerns, assuring us that he would move off the war theme and worrying about himself as a writer. I ended my lecture with statements about our joy in his stories about sharks and sports.

Two days later, Kathleen told me that she had figured out where Tim-Pat's war stories came from while she discussed the American Girl dolls with other mothers at their weekly "play group" meeting. She believed that Tim-Pat was simply interpreting his sister's and her friends' seemingly insatiable fascination with Felicity Merriman, Addy Walker, and Molly McIntire, three American Girl dolls who represent girls' lives during the American War for Independence, the American

Civil War, and World War II. Unable to find common ground with Laura and her friends as they played American Girls, Tim-Pat parlayed admission into their social group (a very important one at our house) by writing *Colonial Times, The Civil War in Texas,* and *World War II*—the American Boy series.

We tested Kathleen's hypothesis by asking both Tim-Pat and Laura. Tim-Pat responded that he had not mentioned this fact because he "wanted to see if you could figure it out yourselves." Laura replied, "Oh, they're companion books for the American Girl stories, Dad." Move over Disney, here comes the Pleasant Company, with thirty books, five dolls, and attendant accessories that gross over seventy-five million dollars per year through catalog sales. But just as powerful as the popular culture veneer of the Pleasant Company is Laura and her friends speaking through Tim-Pat in his books. While the American Girls were having birthdays, going to school, and enjoying spring, Laura, Tim-Pat, and their friends decided that the American Boys must be at war. By treating his stories as simply a personal statement, I applied the wrong curriculum and jeopardized Tim-Pat's understanding of his literacy—"I can make them do anything I want." I missed the multiple ownership of Tim-Pat's stories, ownership shared by Tim-Pat, Laura and her friends, and the Pleasant Company. Moreover, I missed the opportunity to help Tim-Pat (and Laura and her friends) examine the values and social relations that the Pleasant Company authors have put in their heads.

This tracing of apparently individual values, choices, and opinions in people's words and deeds in order to explore their multiple origins broadens the possibilities of the theory of ownership considerably. Acknowledgment of multiple ownership does not end on individual exploration of self and others; rather, it begins our identification and interrogations of our membership in certain groups and a conscious appraisal of what the identities each group has to offer us. When we look at multiple ownership, we often sort through the stories we know. Our lives are connected biologically, historically, and morally. Yet, the stories we learn and tell can either acknowledge these connections or obscure them. Once the multiple ownership is identified, we can examine, argue with, and decide what it is that we hope to stand for and what it is that we once were but which we no longer want to be. Only after we explore the multiple ownership of our words and deeds can we develop intellectual autonomy through sorting out contradicting values, attitudes, and beliefs within them.

Beyond our construction of knowledge and rules for understanding, intellectual autonomy includes the ability and intention to probe who benefits and why they benefit from these constructions. In the development of intellectual autonomy, it is just as important for the Friends School students (and teachers) to reflect upon the processes and messages of the folktale project as it is for them to participate in the project. What does it mean that Quaker principles and popular culture (like Disney) compete within the project? How does the profit motive within the authentic language use influence the project's process and outcome? What social lessons are learned from the negotiation of story and action with four adults? with peers? How does the inclusion of artistic and dramatic as well as literary expression influence which and how students participate and what each takes from the folktale project and its social context?

This type of exploration of multiple ownership (as well as many other types) can help us to expand our intellectual autonomy beyond imbibing the content others teach or knowing how, why, and what to do as experts suggest. If we acknowledge the fact that multiple sets of values and rules for proper behavior, dress, and talk operate within our thoughts, language, and actions and that historical forces influence those choices, then we must understand intellectual autonomy as a political process in which to examine whose stories, values, and interests will be validated within our thoughts and actions and within the social circumstances in which we participate. Politics need not be brought to intellectual autonomy, to literacy, to school, or to ownership. These phenomena are profoundly and fundamentally political. We cannot, nor can children, escape the political impositions of various groups and historical forces within our daily lives. And each group tells us different stories within its agenda for how we should live our lives.

Our intellectual autonomy increases when we challenge the false sense of individualism in the theory of ownership in learning, when we examine the political interests embedded in our words and actions, and when we introduce different ways of living, social organizations, values and ideas to be weighed against those that we already possess. Acting on the fact of multiple ownership can help us to examine the complexities of ourselves and our connections to others and the social and political life that surrounds us. Moreover, it can help us to act in order to make ourselves, our homes, our classrooms, our schools, and our communities more of what we want them to be.

And even children can engage in this practice. When we premiered the folktale video plays in Laura's classroom, these five- and six-year-olds were quick to point out how the endings differed. They spent considerable time trying to identify and analyze what made them different, finally deciding that it had something to do with friendship and commonalities among different types of characters in *Goldilocks and the Three Bears: The Day After*. They appreciated its ending in ways that they could not appreciate the others: "Everybody gets along." "They're not mad anymore." "Everyone eats, not just the pigs" (The pigs ate the wolf at the ending of *Two Pigs and a Wolf*). Tim-Pat, who was five at the time he wrote his stories, discovered on a CD-ROM disk that baseball was invented in 1847 and that some American Boys could have been playing baseball, not making war when Addy Walker was an American Girl. Now *J.C. Invents T-Ball* has replaced *The Civil War in Texas* as his text when he plays "American Children" with Laura and their friends. And Laura, who has accumulated fourteen Barbie dolls from garage sales, inheritance, birthdays, and such during her ten years on earth, was heard to say as she held up Totally Hair Barbie, "What's Mattel trying to say to me with all this hair?"

When we think about what we want for ourselves and for children, it is easy to acknowledge the importance of the ownership of our learning, literacy, and actions. Through this ownership, we expect to find ourselves, to become truthful and authentic, fulfilled and complete. Within this process, voice becomes the recognition of multiple social groups that speak to one another through individuals. Choice becomes the intersection of historical influences within a particular context that effects decisions. Control becomes the negotiation with others to determine whose and what stories will be told and who will do the telling. Authenticity becomes the realization that control, voice, and choice are political phenomena that condition and are conditioned by individual and group action. And intellectual autonomy becomes the evaluation of competing interests that collide within and around us to fashion a social morality that helps us not only to affirm our identities but also to face each other, to investigate our differences, and to decide collectively how we wish to live together in and out of schools.

Chapter 3

Arguing About the Control of Classrooms

*W*hen Laura started kindergarten, she thought she could read and write, and she could. She could read a number of simple books cover to cover, identifying words quite accurately, always substituting words that made sense when she strayed from the text. She wasn't ready for Tolstoy's *War and Peace* by any means, but she could certainly handle Dr. Seuss's *Hop on Pop*. Although she consulted books and magazines to answer questions she had about the world ("How do roller skates work?"), she greatly preferred stories, particularly ones with girl protagonists.

Laura wrote lists of things she wanted to do or remember or, more often, what she wanted her parents to do for her. She wrote thank-you notes and letters under some duress, but she enjoyed writing place cards and agendas for parties and play time because she already realized that controlling the pen meant she had some control over people's actions. Like her reading, her writing was not always adult-like. She invented spellings, commanding all the consonants, but stumbling badly over "short" vowels and silent letters. She spelled to sound, but pronounced some words incorrectly. Because she lacked co-ordination in intricate matters and she wanted to write rapidly "to get on with the game," she used capital letters exclusively. Although capital letters were easier for her to make, she still pointed some of the letters in the wrong direction. But her messages and stories usually made sense, and her family and friends encouraged her frequent writing, acknowledging, and sometimes complying with, her written imperatives.

Laura was literate. She used reading and writing to get things done, to exercise power over others, to maintain personal relationships ("I love you, Mom"), to express herself, to invent and play, to convey information, to find things out, and to evaluate herself, others, and the structure of her world ("Dad, why can you tell me to go to bed when I am not tired?"). She read symbols and rituals as well as print. Laura had attended preschool for three years, and when asked what she expected the first day of kindergarten, she replied, "You know, go through the names and learn the rules." When asked what she hoped for, she declared, "To work on the computers, to have an art corner, and to write our own stories and a turquoise pencil." To prepare for her first day of school, she printed her name on a sheet of paper, cut it out so that it could be fastened to her sweatshirt, and skipped toward the bus with her name tag in her hand.

When she returned home at noon, she held a sheet of paper with her name on it. When we asked her about her day, she suggested that her predictions had been accurate and that there were some "bad" boys in her class who would not follow the rules—"Sit quietly for the opening of the day or wait their turn to get a drink after recess." When we looked at the sheet she brought home with her, it had ⅃ A U Я A toward the top in Laura's printing, followed in her teacher's printing by, *L a u r a*, followed by sixty-three lower case *a*'s in Laura's printing, and concluded with *perfect* written in red ink by her teacher.

It took some prying to get Laura to talk about this sheet. She reported that her teacher had asked if she could write her name. After she had complied, her teacher told her, "We don't write that way at school," demonstrated "the proper way" to print her name, showed her how to print a lower case *a*, and then requested that she practice this letter. (Several days later, Laura brought home a lower case *u* worksheet.) Laura explained that she wrote sixty-three *a*'s because she wanted to show her teacher that she could "do it." When we asked why she wrote ⅃ A U R A in the first place, she said that it was her signature, and she wanted it to be "super deluxe" like Ramona Quimby's signature in *Ramona the Pest* (Ramona Ɋuimby). "Did you tell your teacher that?" "She didn't ask."

This may seem like a simple story about an innocent exchange between a teacher and a student. Perhaps it is typical; certainly it reminded me of my schooling. But this encounter had profound consequences for Laura—she stopped all reading and writing at home after the first day of school—and it encapsulates some of the argument about literacy and learning in at least the United States. Kathleen and I believed sincerely that all our work with literacy and our encouragement of Laura's literacy acquisition had prepared her for school. In one brief exchange, Laura's teacher had demonstrated to Laura the folly of our belief and the inappropriate nature of our literacy for that classroom.

Just as Laura shared the ownership of her ⅃ A U R A with Beverly Cleary (the author of *Ramona the Pest*, 1992, Avon), and her parents and friends, Laura's teacher shared ownership of her name-writing activity and response with many others. While the particulars of her words and actions were her personal choices, those choices fall well within the boundaries of a psychological perspective on literacy and learning. Called *scientific management, effective teaching,* or simply "what works," this approach to schooling stems from the belief that knowledge is assembled the same way as an automobile and that learning is measured like profits and losses in a ledger. In this perspective, the job of teachers, then, is to be good business-people—to produce a standard, quality product (a certifiably literate graduate) at the least cost (in the most academically and instructionally efficient ways).

Business is a compelling metaphor, one that understandably has garnered great support from government and industry and has directed most elementary schools and teachers for the last seventy years. Clearly it influenced Laura's teacher, who began with the best of intentions but who left Laura and real literacy in her wake. Laura's teacher wanted to know if Laura could print letters because, according to psychological perspectives, the correct recognition and printing of letters are the first steps in learning to read and write. To find this out, she gave Laura a test—"Can you write your name?" Because the correctness of the letter formation was paramount, Laura's teacher disregarded the signature aspects of the task and zeroed in on the penmanship. When she identified "error," she brought it to Laura's attention and corrected it, so that Laura wouldn't believe that her rendition of her name was correct printing. Because correct learning requires practice, Laura's teacher demonstrated the shape of a lower case *a* and asked Laura to copy it in isolation. When Laura complied, she wrote *perfect* to reward her. Perhaps the red ink was used to ensure that Laura noticed her reward.

Laura's teacher expected Laura to learn social lessons about schooling as well as the academic ones. First, Laura was expected to learn that teachers set the rules for proper learning and behavior by themselves. That is, the teacher selects the topics, the time, and the place for engagement; the rationales for particular activities; and the criteria for success in school. Second, Laura was supposed to learn that correctness of form is expected from the outset and is more important than personal relevance. Although ⌐ A U R A does spell Laura's name, it does not appear in the school format, and therefore it could not be considered correct. Third, Laura was directed to recognize that her experiences, literary or direct, were of little value unless they coincided with school expectations and procedures. That is, the literacy of her home—using print to take control and to make personal sense—would not help her figure out how to complete assignments in the classroom. According to psychological perspectives these social lessons of "doing school" were at least as important as the academic lesson.

41

Laura's teacher and her school had plans for Laura's learning completely mapped out from kindergarten through sixth grade before she even entered school. They would use the same map for all students. These first steps toward learning to read and write at school would be followed by the teaching of how to recognize and draw other letters, to recognize the sounds associated with letters, to blend those letter sounds to syllables and words, to place those words in grammatical phrases and sentences, to combine those sentences into paragraphs, and finally to arrange and interpret paragraphs into stories, essays, and the like. This additive process would be followed for both reading and writing and would ensure that all students would receive the same skills if they can work their way through the sequence from letters to meaning in a timely fashion. This approach is designed so that the school "products" will have standard equipment, if they make it all the way to the end of the assembly line. Of course, this is stated too baldly. Laura would read books, write stories, sing, act, and recite along her way through elementary school. But what would really count, as she learned her first day, was her ability to perform designated skills "perfectly."

The logic of psychological perspectives on schooling and literacy stem from a series of experiments performed on animals at the turn of the century. Then, psychologist E. L. Thorndike and his associates attempted to encode all of learning into four scientific laws that would describe how new knowledge was composed from skill connections and how teachers could best manage their students' learning environments. Accordingly, most psychologists believed that any complex task, such as reading and writing, was composed of numerous simple skills. Each skill had to be practiced, rewarded, and tested separately and then assembled into the complex behavior. Accordingly, Laura's teacher isolated her attention on lower case *a*'s, required practice, rewarded her with *perfect*, tested *a*'s for a second day, and then moved Laura on to the next skill in teaching her to write her name correctly.

During the 1910s and 1920s, reading experts and psychologists produced guideline materials to direct teachers and students through the many skills they deduced from the complex tasks of reading and writing. In a short time, educational publishers turned these guidelines into the basal reading series industry. These series were (and still are) comprised of graded textbooks, practice books, teachers' manuals, and tests. Basal series have driven reading instruction in over 90 percent of elementary schools for the last fifty years. Basal publishers claim to supply everything teachers need to teach anyone to read and write—the scope and sequence of goals, directions for lessons, practice activities, and tests. Most Americans have worked their way through these graded series: reading about Dick and Jane, filling in the blanks of purple ditto sheets, and completing unit tests to determine if they were ready for the next set of simple skills.

The basal industry is big business, producing sales of more than four hundred million dollars annually. In fact, the publishing houses are so lucrative that they have been the object of many corporate buyouts and takeovers during the 1980s and early 1990s. An industry that once had over one hundred companies vying for the market now has only five publishing houses (Macmillan/McGraw Hill; Harcourt, Brace; Silver Burdett-Ginn; Scott, Foresman; and Houghton Mifflin) controlling over 80 percent of that school reading market. This movement toward oligopoly makes it very difficult and risky for companies to venture into this market because each new addition costs in excess of twenty million dollars just to allow the newcomer to compete for only 20 percent of the market. To maintain their position in the market, established basal publishers stick closely to their original formats.

However, in order to distinguish their products in the competitive market, basal publishing houses have notable psychologists, professors of education, and school administrators to advise them about their wares. That is, publishers hire these experts to represent their basal series at professional conferences and to advise them about which changes will improve their market share. However, publishers do not risk incorporating too many innovations because they will lose more old customers than they will gain new ones. The last great shift by a basal publisher in the 1970s cost it over 75 percent of its market share in one year. Expert advice and innovation since that time have been tempered with sales staff provisos.

To help the school administrators with *their* bottom line of high reading test scores, three basal publishers offer standardized reading achievement tests to their customers: Macmillan/McGraw Hill produces the California Achievement Test, the California Test of Basic Skills, and the SRA; Harcourt, Brace publishes the Metropolitan Achievement Test and the Stanford Achievement Test; and Houghton Mifflin sells the Iowa Test of Basic Skills. These tests are used in most school districts across the United States as an "objective" measure of the effectiveness of school reading programs and student success. The use of a basal religiously and the periodic application of a matched achievement test goes a long way to explain the paradox of the Lake Wobegon effect (according to Garrison Keillor of the radio show *The Prairie Home Companion*, all children are above average in Lake Wobegon). Contrary to statistical possibility, the majority of school districts in the United States claim that their students read above the national average. These numbers help basal publishers sell basals and state and school administrators sell their schools to their constituencies.

With university professors, business, and the state behind her, Laura's teacher felt comfortable applying the academic and social lessons of a psychological perspective during her teaching. Even in the face of this, Laura was unconvinced that the school's definition of literacy was as good as the one she brought with her from home on the first day of school. This became clear to Kathleen and me during Laura's fourth week of school when Laura refused to talk at all about school one day and went directly to sit in her room after descending from the school bus. After many hours and questions Laura confided that her teacher had thrown her first painting away after holding it up before her class and asking, "Class, what's wrong with this picture?" Although Laura said she claimed the picture, it was thrown away because she had violated the class rules by not writing her name on the painting.

When we asked Laura why she was reluctant to tell us about this incident, she said that she was afraid that she had been bad at school and that we would be angry with her. At this point our united front in support of school began to crumble. It's difficult from any perspective to support public humiliation as a teaching tool. After we told Laura that we questioned anyone's right to throw away someone else's work or to ridicule them, Laura told us not to worry because she had a plan. Just the same, Kathleen and I scheduled for the next afternoon our fourth appointment that year with school personnel. That day Laura dismounted her bus with a big smile and displayed her latest painting, which had only her signature, ⅃ A U R A, painted in twelve-inch-high letters. During the meeting with Laura's teacher later that afternoon, Kathleen and I were told that throwing away Laura's painting had been a successful strategy because Laura had signed her next painting. We realized at that point that Laura needed a different environment in which to improve her literacy. Within a week we removed her from that school and enrolled her at State College Friends School.

Laura's definition of literacy differed greatly from her first teacher's definition. While her teacher sought order and precision in Laura's literacy, Laura sought social connection and self-expression in all her encounters with print. Through her choice of signature (Laura could recognize and with some difficulty produce lower case letters), Laura hoped to communicate to her teacher just a little about who she was then and what she could do. At the very least, Laura's signature meant to show her teacher that she was independent, creative, and "well" read. She hoped to be recognized for these traits just as Miss Binney, the kindergarten teacher, recognized

Ramona Quimby in *Ramona the Pest.* Laura's painting response four weeks later demonstrated that she understood that she and her literacy had been rejected that first day of school. She withdrew from literacy rather than submit, and held her overt response off until she received some validation from those who should have supported her all along.

Laura's response proved her literacy and brandished her commitment to a different educational perspective, one with a different set of values, goals, and ways of behaving. Her painting/text showed her implicit knowledge about literacy and text. She used print critically—to affirm herself and family (who "taught" her literacy), to reject her teacher's psychological perspective on literacy, and to act to reinsert her literacy into that classroom. She allowed the text to signify her pain and anger as well as her intention and identity. In accordance with the psychological perspective, Laura's teacher overlooked all of these subtleties of Laura's text as she focused her "attention" exclusively on Laura's compliance with the rule transgression the day before. Despite her teacher's underestimation of Laura's command of literacy, Laura's literate voice was clear—at least to her parents.

Educators aligned with Laura's educational perspective believe that reading and writing develop in the same way as oral language. That is, people acquire reading and writing through immersion in literate environments wherein written language is necessary in order to get needs met, to participate in social life, and to learn about themselves. In such environments, people are "driven" to develop reading and writing in order to survive, and they find this development relatively easy when the purposes for written language are real and clear. This theory holds true for adults acquiring the ability to read and write additional technical languages as well as for young children attempting to make sense of the print and the world that surrounds them. When the reasons for acquiring reading and writing are clear and hold real consequences, people rise to the occasion and develop sufficient control over written language, that is, if they are supported by empathetic, competent readers and writers.

According to this "naturalistic" perspective, people's desire to use language and literacy purposefully outsteps their abilities to command the forms of language while using them. This may be most apparent in babies' first attempts at oral language, but it is just as true as adults try to get control of (or even kindness from) computers. Try as they might, computer companies and software programmers have not been able to make computers as user friendly as family members are to their youngest members. Unlike the family, which can make allowances for babies', young children's, and even adults' approximations of language form, the computer demands mature, adult-like fluency right from the beginning. The family lets you acquire language and literacy, while the computer tries to teach you about computer literacy. Imagine trying to teach a child to speak by demanding adult fluency from the onset: "No, son, *Da* is not correct. Say *father, father.* Would you like to practice *father?* I won't give you your rattle until you say *father.*" If we expected or required adultlike utterances right from the beginning, we would be a society of mutes.

However, when a baby says "Da" or a young child writes *RUDF* (Are you deaf?), the intention is adultlike. Children intend for their oral or written language to have some impact on the world before them. They expect language, oral or written, to work for them. The baby wants his father or he recognizes his father, or he expects to be picked up by his father, or any number of other things. The little boy who wrote *RUDF* to his mother wanted her to stop reading her book and to pay attention to his needs. While they may say or write very little, they mean very much. In a supportive environment, they develop control over sounds and letters, grammar, and rhetorical forms to make their thoughts and needs known in that environment, largely through a process of trial and error. There is no immutable sequence to this development. Sometimes those environments are quite insular and idiosyncratic as

47

when a family invents pet names, a geographic region maintains a dialect or idioms that are confusing to outsiders, or experts talk or write for one another about their discipline. In each case, individuals acquire language and shape it to fit that social environment.

In this way, language and literacy are both personal and social. The purpose for developing either is to ensure that one's needs get met and thoughts get known, but in order to act on those purposes, language and literacy must take place in a social environment. The personal creative forces of the individual push the invention of new language forms, which push language limits and uses. Language in any context then is dynamic. At the same time, social forces push these personal creative languages toward a shared form to allow communication, the exchange of meanings. As individuals attempt to communicate with others outside of these protected environments, the process of language development begins anew —not from the beginning, of course, but the individual must adapt a personal (social) language and literacy to fit this broader context. The failure to adapt can bring humorous or painful consequences—as when a child disregards polite silence to say what's on his mind or when as an adolescent I failed to switch my language code from talking to my friends when talking to my mother.

Laura and most other children have begun to accomplish these complexities before they begin kindergarten. They have acquired a language and literacy that enables them to live in at least two environments—their family and their community. They read the print of advertisements, television, and street signs. They speak and perhaps write in order to denote ownership of objects, to get their needs met, and to make sensible contributions to the life that surrounds them. They are not complete masters of their language and literacy, but then neither are their teachers or parents, who struggle with legal documents, insurance policies, and tax forms and can be rendered apparently illiterate by some esoteric text on specialized topics from postmodern philosophy and quantum mechanics to cyberlit and rap music. To become accomplished readers and writers of any language, we must be immersed in an environment in which reading and writing of that language is necessary for our needs or survival.

Teachers who advocate this naturalistic perspective might begin kindergarten by asking their students to write their names as Laura's teacher did, but they would do so for very different reasons and in different ways than to judge the printing of lower case letters. First, name writing must have a social purpose—perhaps a name tag that would enable teachers and other students to identify who's who in the classroom. By watching them closely as they write their names on the tags, teachers could take note of their students' notions about the conventions of print-type of letters, position, and style as well as their ability to grasp the purpose of the activity. A name tag is a natural reason to write your name—one that Laura intuited before she entered her kindergarten classroom. That tag, brought from home, would tell the naturalistic teacher that Laura, spelled ⅃ A U Я A, was a highly literate being. When that teacher discussed the name tag with Laura, she would learn about Laura's intentions (and pretensions).

Rather than delve immediately into instruction and practice with Laura, this teacher would then look for other contexts in which Laura could write her name purposefully—perhaps to label her coat hook or cubbie (the place where kindergartners keep all their stuff). In this purposeful activity, Laura would be expected to make it clear to all that she occupies this space and that it is reserved for her. In this context, the teacher might expect a different rendition of Laura's name than her name tag, one with less personal expression and more social convention so that it will communicate occupancy to all. A different rendition would demonstrate Laura's understanding of the effect of purpose and context on literacy.

As for the social convention of the distinction of lower case and capital letters, a naturalistic teacher would wait to evaluate that when a context required a differentiation between the two. To my mind, that teacher could wait a long time before the distinction would become naturally important to a kindergartner who writes primarily for himself or his extended family. Should Laura seek a wider audience for her writing, that would be an appropriate time to bring the distinction to her attention by pointing out demonstrations of lower case and capital letter rules. The teacher might present them explicitly to help Laura learn those conventions and when they are useful. In the meantime, Laura would be supported in her attempts to make sense in print in the same way that her oral language was encouraged when she was very young.

Naturalistic teachers don't always wait for their students to stumble into writing or reading conventions. Rather, they set up conditions in the classroom in which students must recognize them in order to make their needs and thoughts known as well as recognize the needs and thoughts of others. These conditions might include the print that surrounds all of us—labels, signs, and lists. The art corner would be labeled so students could put things away in their proper places; there would be a stop and go sign for exiting class to use the toilet; and the day's activities would appear in a list on a bulletin or black board. The production and display of print in these ways builds on the literacy that all students bring to school. They might not recognize all the particular words at first, but they certainly will recognize the uses of print. Moreover, there would be books, places to write, and reasons to write in naturalistic classrooms. Students, even kindergartners, would be expected to accept these invitations to read and write from the very first day of school. Reading and writing would not be taught separately from each other or from other subjects. Instead, they would be incorporated in students' study of themes, and teachers would allot time to discuss the various uses of print to ensure that students learn about language as they study history, science, mathematics, and literature.

A naturalistic perspective presents a different set of social lessons than the ones Laura's teacher intended. First, the environment and the people in that environment must convey to learners that they are capable and deserving of support regardless of their starting point. Since all people are assumed to be literate in some environment, the community of the classroom is charged with helping individuals to build bridges between their home literacy and that of the classroom. Second, learners must recognize that they have choices within the classroom—that they are expected to negotiate what, how, and when events will take place and to accept responsibility for their choices and negotiations. In naturalistic classrooms, teachers and learners form a partnership in curriculum development. Finally, learners must develop and use a personal voice during literacy events. They are expected to interpret all texts, to state their personal case, and to recognize how their voice can be useful in different contexts. That is, learners are expected to see themselves as active individuals ready to participate at some level in any environment. By acquiring these social lessons, naturalistic educators believe themselves prepared to be lifelong learners.

The power base for Laura's perspective is slight in comparison to the business/university/state backing of psychological perspectives. Since teaching from a naturalistic perspective requires libraries, media, and experience—but not textbooks, teachers' manuals, and standardized tests—it has few corporate backers. Recently, basal publishers have cut deeply into the children's literature publishers' interest in the naturalistic perspective by paying high prices for the rights to republish and excerpt literature in basal anthologies. There are some professional teacher organizations—the National Association for the Education of Young Children and the Whole Language Umbrella—and a few state education departments (most notably New York, California, and Pennsylvania) that stand behind Laura and her literacy.

Laura's and her teacher's perspectives are not the only ones that figure prominently in the debates about literacy and schooling in the United States. A third set of perspectives can be found under the newspaper headlines about what Americans don't know, on television when politicians and pundits speak about what's wrong with American schools, and even at

K-Mart. Although I am amused by what editorial-page writers think Americans should worry about and I am almost deaf to politicians' words on any matter, I am drawn to the displays of E. D. Hirsch's Fundamentals of Good Education series (Random) while I shop for soap, toys, and tools at K-Mart. In order to test my knowledge, during every shopping trip I manage to wander by those six books, which tell teachers, parents, and children what every first through sixth grader ought to know. It's amazing what I disremember.

Hirsch, a professor of English, argues that psychological perspectives are too interested in skills and naturalistic perspectives are too preoccupied with self to provide a proper academic foundation for American children. What these perspectives lack, Hirsch suggests, is the intellectual content that will provide a shared background among students that will make schooling "more effective," "more fair and democratic," "more defined and standard," and "more unified and cooperative." Although psychological perspectives prepare students to talk about their abilities and naturalistic perspectives help them develop language and personal insights, cultural literacy perspectives present core information that enables students' talk and action to address matters of consequence. Hirsch's core information is organized within a traditional disciplinary framework: language arts (literature and grammar), civilization (American and world geography and history), fine arts (music, dance, and visual arts), mathematics (not just arithmetic), and science (natural, physical, and chemical). All for ninety dollars.

By defining the core of the elementary school curriculum for all students across the entire nation, advocates of cultural literacy argue that all American children would start with the same basic information about the world and how it works. According to advocates, cultural literacy equates with increased power and opportunity. Currently, they suggest that this knowledge is only available to economic elites who enroll in private schools. Tracking systems of most public schools, like the ones I attended, do not offer this information to middle- and lower-tracked children. However, if every teacher followed a core curriculum, cultural literacy advocates reason, all students would be able to read the culture into which they were born or to which they immigrated. From those readings, they would be able to talk and write about that culture knowledgeably. Later, some may even be able to add to that culture by discovering or inventing new information.

Because of its importance, advocates maintain that core information must be taught explicitly because few families offer the breadth of knowledge and experience cultural literacy requires. The purpose of schooling then becomes providing the core information that will make all students culturally literate. The role of the teacher in this schooling differs from the classroom executive of psychological perspectives or the learning therapist of naturalistic perspectives. Teachers of cultural literacy must be sages who can entice students into highly charged intellectual environments and then initiate them into the world of high culture and academic discipline. In a word, the teacher's job is to "civilize" students in order to make them more human.

This civilizing or humanizing process requires social lessons as well as academic ones. Along with ethical codes of academic disciplines—intellectual honesty, ability to withhold judgment until evidence is weighed, and rigor—comes deference to authority, valuing reason over emotion in all circumstances, and feelings of personal inadequacy that you do not and cannot know enough. In its more popular articulations, cultural literacy is tied directly to socialization to "American ways of thinking" that focuses on unquestioning patriotism, our European heritage, and competition. As former Secretary of Education William Bennett writes, the purpose of cultural literacy perspectives is "to improve America's schools and to affirm the common culture." His definite article, *the*, is intended to connote those American ways of thinking and to promote them to the status of virtues. In his recent books, *The Devaluing of America: The Fight for Our Culture and Our Children* (1992, Summit) and *The Book of Virtues: A Treasure of Great Moral Stories* (1994, Simon & Schuster), Bennett maintains that the academic and social lessons within cultural literacy perspectives are inseparable.

Perhaps the most accessible examples of teachers of cultural literacy can be found in two popular films—*Dead Poets' Society* (1990, Touchstone) and *Stand & Deliver* (1988, Warner). These films present highly regarded teachers working cleverly to evoke and maintain students' interest in poetry and mathematics, respectively. In *Dead Poets' Society*, Robin Williams portrays Mr. Keating, a private preparatory school teacher who wants his students to "seize the day and make your lives extraordinary" by being poets, not just by studying poetry. To initiate them to the life of poets, he tries everything from tearing pages from the tired English textbook to having them stand on their desks in order to sound Walt Whitman's "barbarian yawp." In the end, his teaching is too successful as the poetic lives of his adolescent students run afoul of the authoritarian traditions of the Dalton School.

In *Stand and Deliver*, real-life educator Jamie Escalante (played by Edward James Olmos) quits a high-paying job as a computer designer and programmer to teach. He speaks both Spanish and English to his bilingual students and teaches extra classes during nights and weekends in order to draw high school students from Los Angeles barrios toward calculus. Although *Stand and Deliver* addresses a different population than the *Dead Poet's Society*, student redemption in both films comes through their willingness and abilities to transcend their immediate surroundings in order to enjoy the beauty and to endure the tribulations of the rigor of high-level academic work. In *Stand and Deliver*, initiation into the discipline of mathematics comes only when California Department of Education officials accept the fact that most of Escalante's students passed the Advanced Placement calculus examination.

Although I didn't have Mr. Keating or Jamie Escalante or even Miss Jean Brodie or Mr. Chips as teachers, most of my elementary, junior high, senior high, and college teachers applied various versions of cultural literacy for sixteen years in order to lead me to culture. Their efforts were always earnest, if not always successful. And now I stand in K-Mart looking at Hirsch's books wondering about Laura's and Tim-Pat's chances to become civilized. When I examine the pages that ask six-year-old students to consider Mayan, Aztec, and Incan civilizations and nine-year-olds to study Charlemagne and the Holy Roman Empire, I can hear my former high school teachers' voices asking me to sit up straight and pay attention. Despite my better judgment, I worry that I don't remember all those dates, equations, and formulas. Will my children? Should they?

If some federal government officials have their way, they should and they will. Cultural literacy has been the accepted educational perspective for at least the last fifteen years, covering the Reagan, Bush, and Clinton administrations. Beginning perhaps with Secretary of Education T. H. Bell's creation of the National Commission on Excellence in Education in 1981, the federal government has sponsored a series of reports: *A Nation at Risk* in 1983, *What Works* in 1986, *America's Choice: High Skills or Low Wages* in 1990, *America 2000* in 1991, and the Educate America Act in 1993. The federal position on cultural literacy began by inducing fear.

> Our once unchallenged preeminence in commerce, industry, and technological innovation is being overtaken by competitors throughout the world . . . What was unimaginable a generation ago has begun to occur—others are matching and surpassing our educational attainments. If an unfriendly foreign power had attempted to impose on America the mediocre educational performance that exists today, we might well have viewed it as an act of war.

During the last decade, the federal government with the backing of most state governors has called for and helped implement increased high school standards for graduation, testing for teacher certification, a corporation to finance break-the-mold schools, and numerous financial incentives to encourage schools and teachers to follow core curricula and cultural literacy. These improvements have culminated in *America 2000* and the Educate America Act, which set several national educational goals:

1. All children will be ready to learn when they start school,
2. 90 percent of all students will graduate from all high schools,
3. all students will be competent in core subjects,
4. students' knowledge of mathematics and science will rank first in the world,
5. every adult will be literate and able to compete in the work force, and
6. all schools will be safe, disciplined, and drug free.

According to the reports each of these goals will be met by the turn of the century.

In order to meet the third goal, the Educate America Act established a twenty member National Education Standards and Improvement Council that will develop criteria for approving voluntary national curriculum standards (the federal government has no legal role in setting school standards) establishing what all students should know and be able to do: "The council will certify content standards in each academic discipline, assure that all students have access to these standards, and monitor assessments to measure students' mastery of those standards." With financial inducements from federal government, the professional organizations in English language arts, mathematics, economics, social studies, and science education have completed or are busy writing those standards and tests. Once written they will begin the process of making America a nation of cultural literates.

The real possibility of national standards and tests throws the debates about literacy and schooling into high relief. Because the federal government does not have a legal role in setting school curricula and assessment, it must negotiate those standards and tests with state education departments, professional educational organizations, and school districts. With this primary interest in skills transmission and efficiency, advocates of psychological perspectives are likely to find national standards for curriculum acceptable as long as they can develop the instructional techniques, the textbooks, and the tests. This deal will probably be acceptable to cultural literacy advocates and the federal government. Because of their limited power base, naturalistic advocates are unlikely to figure prominently in the development and implementation of national standards and tests. Those who want to be players in these negotiations are likely to trade content standards for the possibility of including a few standards for the classroom environment and to argue for assessments other than paper and pencil examinations.

In the year 2000, Laura will be fifteen and Tim-Pat will be thirteen. Unless there is an abrupt change in our course, national standards and tests will be in place and will direct the schooling that they are offered. Just what should those standards be and how should we assess whether or not they are being met? Who should be involved in decisions and how should we go about making them? These are questions we must address, if our attempts to remake schools will have a positive impact on our children's and our own lives. Although standards could help us to influence schools' direction and practices and to assess how well schools are helping our children prepare to face the future, we must be careful to avoid replicating mistakes from the past when schools systematically denied many, perhaps most, students access to the knowledge and understanding that led to "the good life" and turned everyone's education into "just taking classes." If we acknowledge that the ways schools work have something to do with how we live together outside of school, then we can't sit back and let the experts take care of academic standards and schools for us. In fact, traditional experts and their expertise can only exacerbate the problems of the past. We need a different direction.

Chapter 4

Changing the Rationale for Schooling

*A*irline travel in the Northeast during January is always an experience. Recently, it took me nine hours to make a one-hour flight to New York City. I live in State College, Pennsylvania, whose unofficial motto is "We're nowhere, but we're close to everywhere"—three hours' drive to Baltimore, three and one half to Pittsburgh, four to Philadelphia, and four and one-half to New York City. To fly anywhere, we must first hop to Pittsburgh, Philadelphia, or—less often—Baltimore. To go to New York City, I had to fly west to go east. On this particular flight, I arrived in Pittsburgh on time at 1:00 P.M. and then started the seemingly endless process of trying to get to New York City when it is snowing in New York. La Guardia Airport, my original destination, was closed.

Although I have a tendency to personalize such circumstances, there were hundreds of travelers who were "stuck" in the Pittsburgh airport. We boarded and then "deplaned" two flights to John F. Kennedy Airport on Long Island. The first flight was canceled while boarding; the second was on the runway when JFK closed. I stood unsuccessfully in the stand by line for two flights to the Newark, New Jersey, airport. I was beginning to feel like a character on *Gilligan's Island*, when my name was called for a third flight to Newark at 9:05. We arrived in Newark at 9:45, and I went to stand in line to wait for a taxi. There were at least one hundred people ahead of me, and I was unfamiliar with the airport bus service to Manhattan. I expected another hour wait. Five minutes after

I reached the line, however, a fellow tapped me on the shoulder and asked "Manhattan? Forty bucks." I would have followed him anywhere, and five others at the end of the line had the same feeling.

Down some stairs, around the back, and through the slush to his unmarked car we all trudged: a woman from Puerto Rico, a man returning from "business," a young woman who stood in line with me in Pittsburgh, a fellow who came to meet her at the airport, and me. We squeezed into the car fairly easily. The driver, businessman, and woman from Puerto Rico in front, the fellow who met the woman between her and me in the back. The fellow who met the plane couldn't stop talking. "What do you all do?" "Oh, my brother does that." "Where are you from?" "Pittsburgh, originally, but Morristown, New Jersey, now." "How long was your flight?" "I've been to all the airports today waiting for *her*." "I had a Russian cab driver, an engineer." "I like to talk, can you tell?"

Finally, his woman friend asked him, "How was business today?" He replied "Business is good. I met with the people at Valley HMO to cut costs." He turned to me. "I like the Clinton health plan. I didn't vote for him. But I like the health plan. Valley must cut their costs. We can do that for them by a factor of ten, and everybody is going to make money here." He touched my arm. "I *like* this plan," he repeated, and then he looked away. "Of course, some clerical workers—a lot actually—are going to lose their jobs." He continued, "Business is good. Are you hungry?" "Yes, I'm starved," his friend replied. I heard nothing else except the driver asking for my destination. I was last to be dropped off, and before I got out, the driver asked me about colleges of engineering where his brother, who just graduated from the University of Cairo, might apply.

This is a rich text, one replete with symbols that can be interpreted to make sense out of and to bring meaning to our lives. What type of literacy, that is, which educational perspective, can help us read this text? Of course, one needs psychological skills to decode and process the symbols of my day and the conversation. As a listener/reader, I must attend and select which stimuli, visual or oral, allow me to make sense of what transpired before me. I must be able to make main ideas from the text at hand and attach details to those main ideas. I did attend to the conversation in the car in ways I'm sure that no other passenger did. For example, the business man's terse retort—"business"—to the question of why he was traveling told me that he wished to be left alone. He was most likely not paying attention at all to the story of the Clinton health plan. That I selected that story among all the topics of this trip (airline deregulation, New York City cab rides, Northeast winters) shows that I can decode symbols, make main ideas, and assign details. At least some skills of a psychological perspective are necessary for reading, but certainly they are not sufficient.

To make sense of this text, I used some information that cultural literacy advocates would call core. I knew some geography, some recent history about airlines, who President Clinton is, and what his health plan might entail. Without this basic knowledge, I would not be able to follow the text. Although even a passing knowledge would allow me to follow the text, the more I know about this information the better sense I can make. For instance, if I could trace the interdisciplinary nature of the fellow's story about his day's work— connecting current events with the sociological makeup of the cab riders and the economics of the new health plan— then I might infer what the other listeners thought about his story's content. With this, I'd be reading the text (his story) and its immediate context (the cab ride). Yet, the meaning I negotiated during that reading would stand apart from me.

Where do I stand in this text? Why were parts of this fellow's answer directed at me? Why did he face me when he said he likes Clinton's health plan? Why did he then touch my arm when he reiterated it? What was it in my appearance, demeanor, or talk that signaled that I would be an advocate of the Clinton plan? How did the day affect my interpretation of the cab ride and this story? How does the Clinton plan affect my family and me? Why didn't it bother me that the cab driver was making two hundred dollars for an hour's drive and it cost 650 dollars to fly two hundred miles? (Before deregulation, the price was ninety dollars.) Answers to these questions are important for a naturalistic personal understanding of this text.

Yet, even the sum of these perspectives seems to leave an inadequate reading of this text. Although sense can be made through sorting the content into main ideas and details in order to develop a personal interpretation, such a reading misses two main points that raise the cab ride text from personal interest to social significance. First, how can *everybody* make money on the Clinton plan if "a lot" of clerical workers will lose their jobs? This paradox can only be eliminated if clerical workers are excluded from the category of everybody. Perhaps this makes them nobodies—people who are beyond or beneath consideration when social and business policies are being considered.

There seem to be a growing number of nobodies across America. According to the U.S. Labor Department, there were 250,000 new layoffs in 1993—that's a quarter of a million new nobodies. Some maintain that current social and business policies turn 40 percent of the U.S. population into nobodies who make a life on only 16 percent of the country's income. In the business section of the *New York Times* the day after my cab ride, GTE announced that it would cut seventeen thousand jobs—14 percent of its work force—over the next three years. Ironically, it's stock value rose with the announcement of the layoffs.

Second, the cab ride suggests that America is a multicultural society. This should not come as a surprise to anyone because America has always been a multicultural society since Columbus brought a second race to its shores. Even before his "discovery," there were Inuit, Iroquois, Mayan, and other cultures inhabiting this hemisphere. While our cab ride did not include the most diverse group in America—you had to have forty dollars in your pocket to get into the cab—we had a gender, racial, ethnic, language, and social class mix. Census demographics suggest that America will become even more diverse over the coming decades. Racial and ethnic minorities are expected to increase to 40 percent of the population by the turn of the century. Immigration is expected to account for over 35 percent of all U.S. population growth. In some urban areas, teachers report as many as seventy different languages spoken in their classrooms. And the gap in income between the rich and poor is the widest it has ever been in this country.

While the cab riders shared the day's struggle against the weather and we shared space for thirty minutes, we did not share the same privileges. Men talked. Actually, one man talked most of the time. Women listened, or filled the role of keeping the monologue going. "How was business today?" Recent immigrants—one Egyptian, one Russian—drove taxicabs. The woman from Puerto Rico apologized for her English. We all listened to a lecture from a businessperson about what's good for America, and we all experienced a young entrepreneur with snow tires demonstrating the maximization of profits. Many cultures, with many different levels of power.

In order to read this cab ride text adequately, I needed a literacy that pushes beyond the skills and content in ways that connect my personal understanding with a social understanding—that is, a literacy that connects me with other people through an ethical and moral stance toward justice. Why should health plans make people money? Isn't health care a basic human right? Who are these nobodies who seem expendable to moneymakers? Why apologize for one's language? Why should women be silent while men speak? These questions that begin ethical and moral connections among people are part of a critical perspective—a fourth position in the debates among psychological, cultural literacy, and naturalistic perspectives about schooling and literacy.

Critical perspectives are based on the premise that the social negotiations of the rules of proper behavior, laws, and social institutions are not conducted among equals because social, economic, and political circumstances (history) have given certain groups license to assert undue influence over the outcomes. For example, the clerical workers were not invited to the meeting to determine how the Clinton health plan was going to affect Valley HMO. They will probably not be party to the decision to lay off workers, although their union may be asked to choose among its members who will leave. This is the new "partnership" between business and labor. The rules of conversation within the cab were not negotiated among equals either. The woman from Puerto Rico felt obligated to answer inane questions, while the businessman could escape with one terse word. Such is the new "equality" between the sexes.

Because these and other societal negotiations are not conducted among equals, the outcomes of those negotiations benefit negotiators unequally. Everybody will make money, except the lesser of equals, the clerical workers. The woman from Puerto Rico apologizes for her use of her second language in order to address a question she doesn't want to answer in the first place, while the speaker continues to tell her about his trips to the Caribbean. In fact, the rules for who can negotiate and how they can negotiate in such matters were established long ago. Because of this, the unequal participation and outcomes seem to follow a natural course of events. "Of course, some clerical workers—a lot actually—are going to lose their jobs." "How was business today? . . . Yes, I'm starved." The inequalities appear benign, appropriate, and "just the way things are." Critical perspectives, however, challenge these and other inequalities as injustices and asks, why are things the way they are?

This seemingly innocent question is both a weapon and a tool. As a weapon, it invites analyses of everyday events in order to investigate how inequalities encoded there are related to the social organizations that affect our lives. Certainly, I look at the cab ride or Laura and Tim-Pat's schooling in order to make personal sense of my life, but I also examine them to discover how federal policy, business, popular culture, and schooling present opportunities and constraints for all of us. When I look at mundane events—first days of school, play among siblings, men and women talking —and ask why things are the way they are, I am attacking the past and present inequalities that pervade our lives. When I ask that question, every word, every act, every gesture becomes problematic.

As a tool, this question makes change seem possible and facilitates action. If I didn't believe change possible, I wouldn't ask the question. To learn about inequalities without believing in a possibility for justice would be an invitation to cynicism. The intent of adopting a critical perspective and asking questions, then, is to illuminate past and current inequalities, to document their consequences on our lives, *and* to identify contradictions within current relations and events as opportunities for change toward more just relations. For example, the everybody/nobody contradiction is an opportunity to discuss fairness in the Clinton health plan. Over time, you begin to see patterns and connections among the inequalities you illuminate. For example, my story about my first few weeks of junior high school from the preface connects with the fellow's story about his day's business because writing off certain sections of the school population into the lower tracks is similar to laying off clerical workers. My son's reading of gender roles in his sister's play surrounding the American Girl stories clearly connects with the conversation patterns during my cab ride. We can't stand apart from these inequalities. We live them daily.

I began this chapter with the story of my cab ride to Manhattan because I believe its two main points identify contradictions in currently popular approaches to school reform and demonstrate why critical perspectives should direct schools of the future. Much of the rhetoric that surrounds calls for school reform suggests that schools do not prepare students properly to enter the workforce and that school curricula should return to "basics" and American "values." Those sentiments are expressed in the national goals of *America 2000* and the Educate America Act—all adults will be able to compete in the workforce and all students will be competent in core subjects. In fact, these goals have provided the rationale for schooling for the last one hundred years—schools are supposed to educate and to socialize children toward work.

Throughout the twentieth century, increased amounts of schooling have generally translated into the increased likelihood of employment at higher wages. Staying in school meant eventually you would receive a credential that would enable you to apply for a better job. In most cases, a better job was defined as one with high wages. Of course until recently, most students who left school could find employment as laborers, on farms, or in factories. (Where those jobs are still available, school dropout rates are substantially higher than in comparable communities.) The wage equations were simple. A grammar school certificate equaled a certain amount of money, a high school diploma equaled so much more, a trade school degree equaled a bit more, and so on up through master's and doctoral degrees. Women and minorities made less at each level, but their ratios remained the same. The adage "Stay in school and get a better job" is all I heard throughout my high school days, and it was pretty good advice.

However, as the clerical workers at Valley HMO found out, the wage equations are not so simple anymore. More schooling does not necessarily equal better pay or even steady employment, but poor schooling is not to blame. The equations don't work anymore because the economy is not producing many jobs with high-level wages nor is it rewarding more education with higher wages. For example, 78 percent of the jobs created by the government, retail business, and service industries since the 1950s pay less than six dollars an hour, which means poverty level income for a family unless coupled with another income. Nearly half of these jobs employ workers for less than forty hours a week, allowing employers to escape paying benefits. During the last decade, manufacturing jobs that pay middle-class wages have declined by 10 percent, and they are expected to fall another 3 to 5 percent during the next decade. The real wages of all workers with all levels of diplomas from grammar to graduate school have declined when compared to the rate of inflation.

When students look at their communities, they do not see high-skill, high-wage jobs waiting for them if only they stay in school long enough to qualify. Instead, they see high levels of youth unemployment, factories closing, and corporations restructuring with fewer employees. The ten jobs with highest demand for workers are food preparation and service, janitors, nurse's aides, orderlies, sales clerks/cashiers, waiters, clerks, nurses, secretaries, and truck drivers. Two recent surveys of workforce skill requirements suggest that employee deportment (no drugs, punctuality, obedience) is the most important and sought-after quality in a worker and that disciplined knowledge (mathematics, natural science, foreign language, and so on) is the least. Better jobs and higher wages can no longer provide the rationale that keeps students in school.

The consequences of the loss of high-wage jobs falls unequally across segments of our multicultural society. Typically, the last hired because of past inequalities—women, racial and ethnic minorities, immigrants, and youth—are the first to face unemployment in high-paying jobs. Consequently, they are the first to be considered for the new jobs without benefits but with poverty-level wages because they have little or no leverage to bargain for more. In rural Pennsylvania where I live, women drive one hour each way to run the cash registers at department stores twenty-four to twenty-eight hours a week for minimum wages. In inner cities there are often fewer opportunities. The unemployment rates for workers between 16 and 21 is nearly three times the national average. And, African American and Latino unemployment for workers twenty-one to thirty-five remains over 40 percent in most large cities.

Traditional explanations for these employment inequalities range from charges of racism, sexism, and ageism to claims

that genetic (intellectual) deficits and cultures of poverty—
absence among poor people of strong family values and the
work ethic—retard the poor and working classes' abilities to
compete for high-wage jobs. Regardless of the sources of
these explanations, calls for school reform seem identical.
Teachers must find ways to motivate students to master the
essentials of the curriculum or students (and America) will
not be competitive in a global economy. Accordingly, *America 2000* and the Educate America Act include the following
goals: all children in America will start school ready to learn,
all children will be competent in core subjects, and every
adult will be able to compete in the workforce. While these
goals appear noble, they leave the problem of succeeding
squarely on the individual who must forsake home, history,
and culture to adopt a "standard" school persona without the
traditional inducement of a job and high wages. For the poor,
this standardization process is to start before school begins
and continue indefinitely into adult life.

Such remedies may have worked when schools could sort
students according to social characteristics and usher them all
toward jobs. Now, schools can no longer conduct business as
usual—not because schools are letting down business by not
preparing workers appropriately, but because the economy is
not prepared to serve most of the population at all well. Only
the children of professional classes are now served at school—
not by the standard fare of core information or skills, but by
the promise of obtaining one of the relatively few high-wage
jobs. The rest must weigh their chances of employment
against the regimentation of school life and consequent
estrangement from family and friends. In this way, the
national goals toward standardization (being ready to learn,
competent in core subjects, and able to compete) work in
direct opposition to the national goal of a 90 percent graduation rate throughout the United States. Why get ready for
school, master esoteric core information, and be ready to
compete for un- or underemployment? Perhaps it is indica-
tive of power relationships in schools and society that at a

time when the links between schooling and work are radically decoupled, government officials, school administrators, and the media are pressing for closer ties with business on the mistaken assumption that the problems of student motivation and achievement could be greatly alleviated if schools articulated themselves in every way with business and industry.

Within a critical perspective, my cab ride serves as a metaphor for these debates about schooling and literacy. The inequalities surrounding employment and social relations within the multicultural microcosm of the cab point to consequences for students as they negotiate their school lives. A few are headed toward the high-wage jobs and may choose to struggle toward the high skills that they require. However, the majority, cutting well up into the middle classes, face a future of tenuous employment in service jobs with poverty wages and limited benefits. National school dropout rates suggest that many high school students recognize this fact. Finally, the contradiction between a health plan to bring universal care and the consequences of clerical workers losing their jobs and health benefits through its implementation parallels a contradiction within a national education policy that sets national goals to prepare all students for high-wage/high-skill jobs when few such jobs exist. By perpetuating the myth that education leads to good jobs, government absolves businesses from responsibility and lays blame for un- and underemployment on individuals.

If the government cannot serve all members of society equally by linking schools with business and industry, then what can the government do with schools to promote equity? My answer is that we should reorganize schools for the purpose of helping students become more active participants in the civic life of their neighborhoods, their communities, and the larger world. If the job culture will no longer be a possible way of defining human value, civic life can become a viable arena in which individuals and groups can seek definition. Moreover, schools directed toward developing civic life will help students develop ethical and moral connections with others. With civic participation at perhaps an all-time low in this country, who can object to such an answer?

Civic life is more than just voting or following local, state, and national politics on television and in the newspaper. It is more than volunteering to help the homeless or sending money to save the Brazilian rainforest. Participating in civic life means joining the struggle to make the world become a more humane and just place in which to live by attempting to come to grips with human diversity and to understand how the world works—warts and all. With a critical perspective and an attitude that questions why things are the way they are, civic life involves affirming some of our social negotiations, artifacts, and instructions and contesting others within our immediate and distant relationships with other people. Through these acts, we affirm and contest parts of ourselves as well. Learning to participate in civic life doesn't just happen naturally, however. If we deem it desirable, then we must organize schools to provide these experiences on some more basic, simplified level. They will allow students to develop the civic thoughts, attitudes, and acts that they will use later in society at large. Perhaps an extended example will make this point clearer.

Although thirty thousand people live in State College, it's still a small town with a mile and a half of stores, restaurants, and parking lots on two streets. Two years ago, Wal-Mart decided to build a store just across the township line. This announcement was treated like the second coming in the local paper because Wal-Mart would bring retail competition and jobs to a region that could use both. Headlines on the front page of the *Centre Daily Times* chronicled Wal-Mart's land purchase, zoning changes, excavation, and construction. Periodically for several months before it opened, *Wal-Mart* was plastered all over the back page of the front section counting the days until the grand opening and explaining why Sam's way (the owner, Sam Walton) was good for customers, employees, and the community.

As Wal-Mart went up, so did a strip mall next to it and a McDonalds adjacent to that. I don't want to make it sound like nothing happens in State College, but all this activity caused quite a stir. The newspaper campaign created a frenzy among some locals, so much so that days before the official grand opening, the parking lot was crowded with the cars of people who noticed that Wal-Mart had already opened its doors. Yes, Kathleen and I did stop in. During the grand opening and every weekend since the parking lots and stores have been jammed with customers. The Wal-Mart is enormous, with merchandise piled to the ceiling, a pharmacy, restaurant (of sorts), and a film center. The strip mall attracted discount shoe and clothing stores, a pet store, a pharmacy, a hair salon, a franchised optometrist, a book store, and restaurants. Even the local grocery store abandoned its building nearby and joined this complex, bringing another pharmacy, another restaurant, a bank, and a bakery.

This Wal-Mart curriculum is too fertile to ignore. It invites students to explore much of modern life. And it does so at multiple levels so that preschoolers to postsecondary students can learn a great deal. For example, Tim-Pat knew right from the beginning that he would find different and less-expensive toys at Wal-Mart than he did at The Growing Tree downtown. At Wal-Mart, he found Ninja Turtles, Bucky O'Hares and X Men, while downtown he found painted metal knights and soldiers. "The Turtles are even cheaper here than at the mall!" he exclaimed. I learned that Wal-Mart was more than a store for many of its customers who came for the day from fifty miles away to shop, but also to eat and to visit. Seldom do these families visit downtown State College in this way, much to the merchants' and restaurant owners' dismay. There are sociological as well as economic lessons to be learned at Wal-Mart.

But there's more. The Wal-Mart curriculum allows for everything from *A* (the elementary study of architecture with its painted bricks and flat roof) to *Z* (the zoo-psychology of the rodents it keeps in tiny cages) with *M* (graduate courses in marketing) in between. And there's depth as well as breadth in every subject. For example, all of mathematics may be studied: arithmetic in all its forms from counting change to dividing microwaved pizza, algebra for tracking the inventory of merchandise, geometry for determining shopping patterns or fresh air flow, and perhaps even calculus. But I can't remember how calculus would be useful at Wal-Mart even after two courses in college.

You can study history through the Wal-Mart curriculum. The history of the site on which the building now stands as well as the history of the company—officially through Sam Walton's biography or unofficially through the business magazine reports on how it grew from a country store to America's largest retailer. Moreover, you could study the historical context that allowed such growth. During its history in State College, it has had considerable impact on the stores downtown—both psychological and real. There's even mystery—I've always wondered why Wal-Mart sits right across the College township line. Ethical duplicity is also a consideration since Wal-Mart's "buy American" campaign was exposed as a hoax by television's *Sixty Minutes*.

Of course, a Wal-Mart curriculum could be studied for a variety of purposes. For example, advocates of a psychological perspective might assign students to visit Wal-Mart in order to apply skills that they were taught, had practiced, and had been tested on. "The next time you visit Wal-Mart, class, comparison shop. Then you'll understand the purpose of four-digit subtraction with decimal points." Older students might be sent there on work/school arrangements to be taught about the world of work. Naturalistic educators could use Wal-Mart as a site for authentic inquiry. Any or all of the ideas I mentioned could serve naturalistic explorations that would develop students' skills and knowledge. For all of these purposes, the Wal-Mart curriculum could be transported anywhere in the country, and of course almost any other value-department store could be substituted for Wal-Mart.

However, to take up the Wal-Mart curriculum for the purposes of developing active participation in civic life would mean something quite different. First and foremost, the civic study of Wal-Mart must be embedded within a specific community setting: What does it mean that Wal-Mart came to State College? This stance on the study would not preclude any topic from being investigated; however, it would direct all students to consider the results of their study within the ethical and moral connections among the people of State College and its surrounding area. Comparison shopping, then, assumes a larger social purpose than simple skill application. Prices would be compared to verify the perceptions of most shoppers. Although lower prices may be a boon to consumers, they do not have straightforward and simple effects on a community. Civic-minded students would ask why the prices are lower at Wal-Mart on some products and not on others and how the buying power of a modern corporate giant effects local shopkeepers within a fifty-mile radius of State College.

In this study, students would learn about the trade-offs of Wal-Mart coming to State College. Certainly, Wal-Mart offers competition for other retail stores in our area. Wal-Mart's prices are lower on many goods, it seems. It brought nearly two hundred jobs to our community for this store alone, and even more when you count the stores that surround it. Wal-Mart has been so successful in State College that its corporate board will build another Wal-Mart and a Sam's Club (a Wal-Mart wholesale members-only store) on the other side of town, and that board just purchased thirty-five acres adjacent to our enclosed mall. These are all positive outcomes for individuals and the communities involved.

However, not all the outcomes are necessarily positive. The Wal-Mart was and the new ones will be built by a non-union construction company from Tennessee. The managers and high-level jobs in the current store are the only forty-hour-a-week jobs, the only ones with health benefits, and the only ones that pay much more than six dollars an hour. Wal-Mart has further centralized retail sales in our region to the detriment of stores in local communities. Many of these stores have cut back on employees or closed because of Wal-Mart's competition. The sum total of new jobs, then, must be reduced by the number of people who lost employment in their local towns. When students figure employment numbers they should keep in mind not just the sales staff but the fewer janitors, delivery personnel, and shelf stockers as well. Certainly, seven or eight hundred cars in the parking lot at any given time do little to improve the traffic patterns in State College. Their exhaust further diminishes the quality of air in our region. There are trade-offs.

A civic study of the Wal-Mart curriculum presents students with the complexities of social life and makes them privy to the pragmatic decisions that local officials and residents must make when deciding how to plan their communities. The students become aware of the competing interests involved. These decisions don't always end with the giant corporations winning. When our family lived in Toronto, we were part of a community that resisted large retail and grocery stores in order to keep our neighborhood stores in business. This meant spending considerably more money for some items like soap and paper products in order that four corner stores, two restaurants, a dry cleaner, and other family businesses could keep their doors open. In return, these families knew our names (they celebrated when Tim-Pat was born); they stocked their shelves with what the neighborhood wanted (the Chinese family who were the new owners of the DiLallo Brothers corner grocery stocked the best Italian bread right next to the bags of rice); and they kept our neighborhood alive and vital. We could walk to all these stores. Students studying the Wal-Mart curriculum should also investigate these types of communities to consider different sets of trade-offs available to us.

Changing economic times require that we change our rationales and metaphors for schooling. Schooling for work or schools organized according to business principles will no longer serve the majority of Americans—even in the unequal ways they did in the past. Rather, schools can serve Americans equally only if we reorganize them to promote students' civic participation in a multicultural democracy. Facing this reality calls into question all of schooling, from the national goals of *America 2000* and the Educate America Act to the classroom practices in local schools. They must all be remade to provide students experiences that will allow them to develop civic courage and responsibility that they will use later. Changes are needed in schools in order to prepare *them* to serve all of society. These changes will put America back to work—the work ahead of us in making our communities, nation, and world a more humane and just place in which to live.

Chapter 5

Understanding Critical Literacy

When Laura was three, she and Kathleen attended a "doll day" held at the Congdon Mansion Museum in Duluth, Minnesota, where we lived at that time. The invitation, printed in the newspaper, requested that each child bring a favorite doll. Laura spent considerable time talking with us about which one of her dolls was her favorite. She declared that it was a difficult selection because different dolls served different purposes for her. Raggedy Ann was for hugging on trips and in bed. Her mother's "saved" Barbies were for story play. A Cabbage Patch Premie, that we bought her when Tim-Pat was born because some psychologists believed that a doll would help a child deal with "displacement" by a new sibling, lay in its basket serving no purpose at all. And her porcelain doll, which her grandmother gave her as a Christmas gift, sat on a shelf to be looked at. Laura decided finally to take the porcelain doll because it had the allure of being out of her reach and Laura reasoned that her grandmother thought Rose was special so she was special to Laura also.

Laura reported with a sad face when she returned that the party was "fun." There had been cake, punch, and games. Women displayed their collections of dolls, doll clothing, and other doll accessories. The gardens around the mansion were lovely, but Laura and Kathleen chose not to wait in a "too long" line to tour the interior. The party's organizers decided that prizes should be awarded in certain competitions. During the party, Laura stood in line to present Rose to the judges so that they could pass judgment on whether she was the oldest, smallest, tallest, most unique, or best-loved doll at the party. Apparently, Rose wasn't old, small, tall, or unique enough among the other dolls being presented, and she lost those competitions. Even Laura could understand why Rose might lose in these categories. However, she wondered aloud how the judges knew how much she loved her doll and her grandmother who had given it to her.

Although I'm projecting, I assume that the party organizers used "best loved" as a euphemism for worn or mussed. While this may be true, Laura interpreted the judges' decision as a declaration that she didn't love her doll as much as the winner loved hers. Laura was disappointed to lose the age, size, and uniqueness competitions, but she was crushed when the judges defined her emotional relationship with her doll as inadequate. "How could I love Rose more?" she wondered aloud. No matter how much Kathleen and I reassured Laura that we knew she loved Rose regardless of the outcome of the competition, Laura carried Rose around for a couple of days—and six years later, she remembered all the details of this event when I checked them with her while writing this chapter. A life lesson learned well.

Our lives are based on competition. We compete for jobs, to keep jobs, to sell more, to look younger, fitter, stronger, to own more . . . More is better, except in golf, body weight, and production costs, and then, less is more, and more is better. We compete even when we are not aware that we are in competitions because when everything in life has a price, we compete just to stay alive. Take our health care system, for example. Pregnant women must compete just to have healthy babies. We have winners and losers in all these competitions, and to the victors go the spoils. To win competitions means material gain, social prestige, and psychological satisfaction. Each win means more gain, prestige, and satisfaction. And more is better, so winning is better. To lose is to gain nothing, which makes losers nothing in a society built on competition.

Schools are based on competition in order supposedly to ready children for the competitions they will face in the real world. Competition pervades every aspect of schooling. School districts compete for state and federal funds, the size and aesthetics of their buildings, and test scores. Schools compete with each other in a district to establish advantageous enrollment boundaries, budgets, and test scores. Teachers within schools compete to garner materials and supplies, to win the respect of parents and students, and for test scores. Grading is based on competition among students; ability groups are arranged to manage that competition so that more students can feel like winners; and even teachers' attention is an object of competition in classrooms with thirty or more students. At the very least, schools reinforce the social ethos of competition, and they influence students' perceptions of themselves as winners or losers.

Even with all this competition in schools, some prominent media pundits and think-tank scholars hope to increase the competition among and within schools through legislation to allow public funds for education to be allotted to individual families so that they might choose which school—public or private—their children attend. The "school choice" movement challenges the state monopoly over elementary and secondary schooling, which according to advocates is responsible for the United States losing its competitive edge in the world economy. That is, American business and industry can't compete economically because our schools lack competitions in learning to hone students' capabilities. Perhaps the most public examples of this concern are based on the fact that American students haven't faired well in international competitions for mathematics and science achievement test scores. Thus, *America 2000* and the Educate America Act state that we will be first in these competitions by the turn of the century.

Although competition may be important in the economy, it is problematic as an incentive to learn better. What does it mean to be a winner at learning? Winners are judged by some external criteria set by anyone other than the learner. If you answer more of someone else's questions, score higher on someone else's test, or complete more of someone else's assignments according to their specifications, then you will be considered a learning winner over your peers. Under these circumstances, the goal of such schooling is to do more of someone else's bidding. This separates learners from their learning because they control neither its content nor its consequences. In classrooms that feature learning competitions, learning is about winning—about gains, prestige, and satisfaction. It has more to do with ego involvement than with performance, coming to know yourself, your own and other cultures, and the workings of the world. While learning competitions may prepare some children for certain aspects of the school of hard knocks to follow, it also ensures that hard knocks is all that will follow for most of the school population.

And what about the losers in learning competitions? How can we define losing at learning? If winning is everything, then losing must be nothing. Although the adage suggests that "It's not whether you win or lose, but how you play the game," children learn quickly in school that most teachers keep score and that it's winning that matters. They just look at the names at the top of the academic lists, the complexions in the top ability groups, and the bodies picked first for sports teams or homecoming queen in order to recognize what really counts in the classroom and on the playground. Just as winning defines the gains, prestige, and satisfaction of winners, losing defines the same for losers. Because of the learning competition, losers seem unable to learn, to think, and to do.

With a steady diet of losing during learning competitions, losers begin to believe that the traits ascribed to them are true. They doubt their abilities to learn, think, or do, and they begin to avoid situations in which they appear to have a personal stake in the direct and subtle competitions. They misspell the first word in a spelling bee to show their contempt. They choose simple books regardless of content in who-can-read-the-most contests because the others are "too hard." They watch instead of participate on the playground. They "hate" math. The stigma of losing learning competitions and the social consequences of those losses affects losers' conception of what it means to know something, their views about what's worth knowing, and their image of themselves, all of which affect their performance at school. Saddled with these confusions and doubts during learning competitions, losers continue to lose, sinking lower in academic standings, in their interest in schooling, and in self-respect.

Learning competitions position students and teachers. They turn students into winners and losers and distort the real accomplishments in and out of a classroom. Competition pits students against one another and the teacher. Other students become threats to an individual's well-being because their gains are her losses as all compete for limited external recognition. Isolated from one another, students cling to a subset of students within their class along superficial lines, claiming superiority to all other groups or individuals on the basis of winning on academic, physical, spiritual, material, or even geographic grounds. Because teachers play the role of arbiters in, at least, the academic competitions, they are forced to exist in the classroom apart from their students. And because each teacher competes with others within a school, they live a similar fate as their students among their peers.

The teachers and administrators at the Friends School that Laura and Tim-Pat attend discussed the effects of competition on learning and learners some time ago. Because they believed that learning should be performance oriented rather than ego involved and that all learners can learn, think, and do, they eliminated formal competition from their lessons and school. There are no grades, no ability groups, and no tests. There are no charts posted on bulletin boards that show who has spelled the most words correctly, read the most books, or showed the best deportment. Classroom privileges rotate according to a published schedule. Anyone who desires to join the choir or play the recorder can practice and perform. Collaboration during lessons and projects is encouraged. Students are encouraged to think that they are "in this together" because every student is responsible to ensure that every student learns the task, information, or rule. Lessons are not finished until everyone "gets it." Winning isn't important; learning is.

This does not mean that the school has few expectations or low standards—that students do whatever they please. On the contrary, individual student performances receive close teacher attention. For example, Teacher Jill asks Laura to look longer into the mirror when drawing her self-portrait during the study of Picasso. She helps Laura think about what she sees and how she wishes to represent it with her pencils. There is no comparison to Picasso except to show that his self-portraits were frequent and changing. No one compares Laura's artistic decisions with those of her classmates. When Tim-Pat picks a book during reading workshop and sits in a rocker, he doesn't worry that Drew's book is thicker or that Jasmine's has fewer or more words. TE listens to him read and supports his efforts to make sense of the texts he chooses by talking to him about them and by asking how those texts help him address questions he has about himself and the world. Even though he can't read all the words, Tim-Pat eagerly uses the classroom encyclopedia to support his report on seals. Learning challenges are evident daily, but learning competitions are not.

However, the Friends School is in competition for students with other schools in this area. When the school's board of trustees, administrators, and teachers considered extending the school beyond the fourth grade, they reconsidered competition in their school because some parents thought the school was too protective of students by not preparing them for public school and later life and because a survey of fourth-grade students at Friends and recent graduates revealed that older students were concerned about the lack of a physical education curriculum.

When the school decided to include fifth and sixth grades, they hired a part-time physical education teacher and charged her with bringing competition to the Friends School. Sports would be the only place where competition was sanctioned, even promoted. Students would experience "the thrill of victory and the agony of defeat" as Jim Mackay announced at the beginning of the *Wide World of Sports* when I was a kid. Gym class would be ego involved, while the rest of the school day would remain performance based.

Laura was a second grader when these decisions were made to expand the school and the curriculum. Sports were an immediate concern for her. She was last to be picked and often found ways to lose games for her team. She reminded me of myself when I was her age. My dad would say, "Pat, it's not that you're slow; it's that you run too long in the same place." (And it was not just my feet that were slow.) Competition was/is not a good motivator for Laura in physical education. She's a loser in sports learning competitions. Although she can swim, jump rope, ride a bike, roller blade, catch and hit a ball, and do jun fan (Bruce Lee's martial arts) outside of school, she quickly developed a negative image of herself as an athlete in school, tried to avoid gym class, and complained loudly to anyone who would listen that she didn't enjoy going to school on gym days.

Laura didn't take long to uncover the paradox concerning competition within the Friends School. Why was it acceptable to compete—to win or lose—in gym class but not in the classroom? She voiced her feelings of inadequacy in gym class, noting that others were faster, more nimble, and more interested in sports than she was. "It's not fair," she would say, "because some people start out better at sports than others. They are picked first every time, and their team always wins." Laura thought about this issue for weeks before she decided to write a letter to the head of the school with her concerns (see Figure 1).

Laura's letter asks Teacher Lee critical questions: Why are things the way they are in this school? Why is competition allowed in one area and not in others? How is it different to be a loser during gym class, than art or reading workshop? She challenges the quick-fix solution of limiting competition

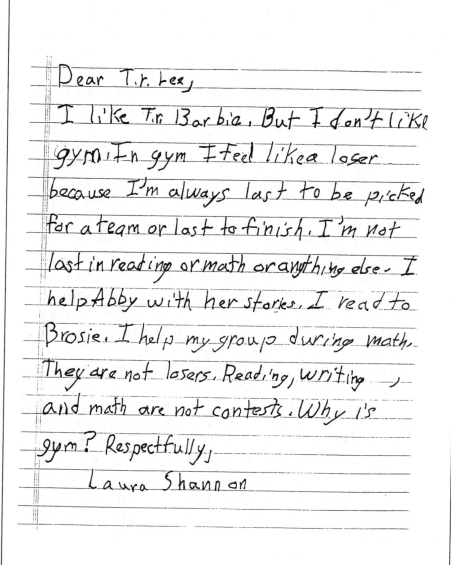

Dear T.r. Lex,
I like T.r. Barbie. But I don't like gym. In gym I feel like a loser because I'm always last to be picked for a team or last to finish. I'm not last in reading or math or anything else. I help Abby with her stories. I read to Brosie. I help my group during math. They are not losers. Reading, writing, and math are not contests. Why is gym? Respectfully,
Laura Shannon

Figure 1   *Laura's Letter*

arbitrarily to one segment of the school day. She discusses the real consequences for winning and losing for herself during gym as well as for others during other parts of the school day if competition were to be expanded to the rest of the school day. In short, she implies that the competition policy is arbitrary, biased, and hurtful and asks the head of the school to think of new metaphors for physical education that will complement, not contradict, the metaphor operating during language arts, science, social studies, art, mathematics, music, and foreign language classes.

This letter demonstrates a change in Laura's definition of literacy from the time she started school. Clearly she still saw literacy as a means to express herself and to make social connections. She certainly wrote what was on her mind, and she felt comfortable enough within the school to ask her questions. But with this letter, Laura moved past her "in your face" ⅃ A U R A as a response to the psychological perspective during her twentieth day of kindergarten. Her letter demonstrated that she would use literacy to make herself vulnerable in order to learn more about herself ("I am not a loser regardless of what the learning competition results may be."), to link herself to others ("If there were competitions in reading, I would be a winner and others would feel like losers. But they wouldn't really be losers either."), and to act by writing the letter. Her use of literacy is well within the parameters of a critical perspective, facilitating Laura's active participation in the civic life of her school.

Critical perspectives push the definition of literacy beyond traditional decoding or encoding of words in order to reproduce the meaning of text or society until it becomes a means for understanding one's own history and culture, to recognize connections between one's life and the social structure, to believe that change in one's life, and the lives of others and society are possible as well as desirable, and to act on this new knowledge in order to foster equal and just participation in all the decisions that affect and control our lives. Because subtle and direct competitions pervade and influence our lives

adversely, much of critical literacy is aimed at naming, ana-
lyzing, and acting upon inappropriate competitions and their
consequences on those lives. Critical literacy helps us assuage
the psychological and social damage not through escape or
denial but by allowing us to ask who benefits ultimately from
these competitions, to forge bonds with our putative competitors, and to work symbolically and physically to ensure more
humane, just, and equitable civic lives.

While Laura's letter may seem inconsequential when compared to this formal definition, her efforts were clearly a demonstration of critical literacy through her exploration of self
and family, her efforts to find connections between her personal feelings and how others must feel as losers in other
types of competitions, her implied revelation that competitions are established by the powerful arbitrarily in order to
simplify the complexity of social issues, her belief that she and
others would be better off if things changed, and her act of
civic courage to question established authority and the status
quo at school.

In her letter, Laura refuses to be positioned by school
competitions and the decisions of the head of school and others. She declares that neither she nor her classmates are losers. Rather, they are different, and it is only the artificial circumstances of competition in which they find themselves that
tries to pin the loser label on them. According to Laura, she's
not a loser or a winner. She's different from her classmates,
who differ from each other. However, the sports learning
competitions reduce each student to a single dimension, and
then define difference on that dimension as winning or losing. Laura implies that this intolerance of difference cannot
be remedied simply by extending the scope of the competition—to include academic learning competitions. Each
competition reduces the differences among her classmates to
single factors. A simple summation of these learning competitions to determine a grade—like a gymnast's all-around
competition or deriving a social studies grade for a report

card—still is a reduction of human complexity and it does not actually accommodate difference. Laura's request was not a personal complaint—"I'm different. Give me a chance to win." Instead, she wanted the school to embrace the differences among her classmates without artificially privileging any particular forms of difference over others through arbitrary competitions. Laura understood the sports learning competitions as an attempt to position difference, one that contradicted the school's stance on academic and social learning.

In effect, the school stance against competition in academic and social learning enabled Laura to note this contradiction presented in gym class. Moreover, its stance on literacy helped her to name the contradiction in ways that other perspectives on literacy could not. For example, a psychological perspective on literacy is based on assumptions that difference from agreed-upon skills and acting skillfully are deficits to be overcome through instruction. Those decisions concerning agreed-upon skills and acting skillfully are made only after human complexities are reduced to single factors (such as a skilled reader of print) or sums of single factors (a skilled student of school curricula). Accordingly, students possessing different skills are not just different, they are considered deficient, at risk, and even learning disabled depending on whom you listen to. The instructional remedies for these losers are supposed to replace students' naturally different skills and to make the students whole, normal, or good.

Psychological literacy education organizes students to compete for reading and writing skills and skillful reading and writing. A scope and sequence of the skills and operational definitions of skillful acts are arranged in a curriculum covering the first seven years of schooling from kindergarten until sixth grade with learning competitions decided through lesson, unit, book, district, state, and—soon—national tests. Students working their way through the preliminary heats of these skill tests become seasoned competitors in a very short time. Moreover, they learn that learning is competition and that literacy is the employment of sanction skills within proscribed circumstances. A psychological perspective, then, positions students and teachers to see differences as deficits and to use literacy within parameters that others set for them.

Cultural literacy begins with a prescribed set of knowledge that all students are expected to learn. The titles of the most popular books from this perspective demonstrate its competitive essence: *What Every American Needs to Know*, *Winning the Brain Race*, and *We Must Take Charge*. In this perspective, students traverse the curricula of academic disciplines with those who most closely approximate what curriculum designers deem essential being labeled "the winners." Those students possessing different knowledge or interests, regardless of their depth, are considered barbarians, incorrigibles, even threats to the well-being of the country.

Ironically, it doesn't really matter what knowledge is agreed upon in a cultural literacy curriculum. Under any set curriculum there must be winners and losers. For example, current curricula in the humanities favor European history and influences, privileging Americans of European descent over Asian Americans, African Americans, Hispanic Americans and Native Americans; curricula in math and science favor men over women. As Laura implied, simply to extend the set curricula to include underrepresented histories and interests would do nothing to end learning competitions and to help everyone appreciate different types and ways of knowing and living. Although shifting the complexion, gender, and social class of the winners in academic learning competitions is appealing, a set curriculum of any sort necessitates ego involvement over performance in the regard for human differences. Here, difference remains a threat to whatever group holds itself to be the starting point for curriculum development and, later, test comparisons.

In this way, cultural literacy positions students to use literacy to excavate the past but also to ignore their own present and its relationship to the past and future. Even the so-called winners in cultural literacy education do not learn about themselves in any real depth. Nor are they asked to construct how they became winners by accident of birth and past negotiations of power. Losers remain losers regardless of their control of literacy or knowledge because they retain the stigma of difference and distance from the accepted academic and social curricula. In effect, cultural literacy works against human diversity by privileging one set of knowledge over all others and establishing literacy as a process of accumulating a standard culture.

At the Friends School, difference is difference. It's not deficit, pathology, or moral failure. It's just difference. Although teachers don't go out of their way to create differences, they do accept the differences in language, culture, knowledge, and ability throughout most of the day. They nurture the individual while attempting to evoke a community spirit at the same time—a delicate balance. The naturalistic literacy program at Friends offers individuals control over the choice of books and writing topics and begins with the assumptions that all of the students are literate, that they learned their literacies in different ways, that they possess different interests and backgrounds, and that those differences are advantages to the literacy program, classroom community, and the school. The Friends School is a place to be different within a literacy program that invites students to explore themselves.

This naturalistic perspective enabled Laura to acknowledge her difference in gym class, and perhaps to use literacy to help her to understand herself. However, the literacy program did not help her analyze the situation beyond the level of her discomfort within that class. For example, the self-selection of literature within that program has meant that she has read mostly fiction with an occasional biography. Her writings at school have been personal narratives, adventures, or mysteries. Although she has read and written often and has made good choices for pleasure or the pursuit of specific information tied to class themes, those acts and choices have never been discussed to enable Laura to examine her understanding of how those texts and that information related to her life beyond her thoughts and feelings.

While the naturalistic literacy program at Friends School was noncompetitive and embraced individual differences, it positioned students to see literacy as a personal and contemplative matter. Accordingly, Laura was able to name and describe her personal response to competition in gym class—to elaborate her thoughts and feelings. However, the literacy program did not prepare or even allow her to identify the contradiction between the academic and physical education curricula at Friends School, to connect her concerns with the broader context of participants in other possible competitions, and to explore the historical context in which competitions become arbitrary expressions of power. Moreover, the naturalistic literacy education did not offer Laura a language with which to do something with her new knowledge—that is, to act in hopes of making things more humane in her civic life.

Critical perspectives on literacy education, which unfortunately Laura and Tim-Pat are only receiving at home at this moment, positioned Laura to see the liberating and activist sides of literacy. She recognized that literacy is a way for her to come to understand herself, her culture, others, and the social structure and to act on each of those issues to make our lives better—more fair, more just, more equal, more free. A critical literacy education provides her with a language of critique in which she can explore the personal and social consequences of learning competitions and to see how competitions are used to isolate and depreciate human differences. It also provides her with a language of hope that enables her to believe that our lives could be different and to work strategically to make change happen. Critical literacy is not only a tool for understanding and change, it's a mindset.

As I am writing this chapter, our part of the world is experiencing its worst winter ever on record—the coldest temperatures and the most snow. Theoretically, such a winter should be good for writing; practically, it has been bad for my back.

Our family has grabbed every opportunity to escape our house in which we have been trapped at least once a week by snow since the start of the new year. It's now the ides of March. During a recent walk downtown, Laura noticed the Greek letters that adorn the windows of the university dormitories facing the main street. She asked Kathleen to explain these symbols to her. The explanation is not straightforward.

Those letters designate the parts of the dormitories in which sororities are housed. The Greek letters on the brick and stone mansions around State College are the designators of fraternities. Laura wanted to know why the women were housed on campus while the men occupied several blocks in town. Kathleen explained that there was a town ordinance to prevent three unrelated women from living together in the same house, and dormitories are not considered houses. Thus, unlike fraternities, sororities must be established in dormitories. This, the town fathers and mothers thought, would prevent the establishment of brothels in State College. Although nine-year-old Laura was not certain what a brothel was, she did recognize the insult to women and the unfairness of the ordinance that she conveyed in her response: "I hope it stays that way until I get to college, then I'll have something to fight against." With her doll still tucked under her arm, Laura knows that life could be different and that she has the right and responsibility to act. That is, she is critically literate—perhaps for life.

Laura's new position on literacy places her within a distinguished history within American education. When led by teachers who demonstrated the power of critical literacy, students of all ages have learned to read, write, and act in the world in order to make it a better place in which to live. In each instance, teachers and students would not simply accept others' definitions, decisions, and control without question. They would not be objects of power. Rather, they learned to use the alphabet and other symbols to establish their positions as subjects in the ongoing negotiations of their lives in and outside of their classrooms.

For example, primary-grade children in Quincy, Massachusetts during the 1880s read books and their community in order to understand why there were so few Native Americans in their area when two hundred years before there had been many. In Chicago at the turn of the century, intermediate-grade students were able to read their community and the newspapers in order to determine how industrial technology in the weaving trades affected different social strata unequally, causing strife for weavers and their families and benefits for plant owners and consumers. In rural Missouri fifteen years later, grade-school children were able "to book" their way to solve typhoid problems among local farmers, to build prototype flycatchers for farm use, and to plan a community health cooperative.

During the 1920s and 1930s at the Work Peoples College in Duluth, Minnesota, recent immigrants, farmers, and their families learned about the advantages of organized labor and political action through the Farm/Labor Party. In the late 1930s, students at the Little Red Schoolhouse in New York City wrote about the homeless and the horrors of war. Throughout the southeastern United States during the 1950s and early 1960s, disenfranchised African Americans learned to read the U.S. Constitution in Citizenship Schools in order to pass the Jim Crow literacy tests for voter registration and through their actions wrote an end to legal apartheid in America. Today, with the leadership of the teacher and parent organization Rethinking Schools from Milwaukee, Wisconsin, children across the country read and write about what it means that Columbus "discovered" an already inhabited hemisphere.

This partial list of examples provides some indication of how critical educators address the skills and content of traditional schooling. While they acknowledge that students must decode print, calculate, think scientifically and historically, as well as know some science and history, they harness those skills and that content in order to illuminate injustices and inequalities in the participation of making and benefits from social and political decisions, to document their consequences for different sectors of society, and to identify contradictions in current policies and practices as opportunities to redress those inequalities and injustices. In short, critical educators organize school experiences to position all students to use their skills and knowledge as Laura did when discussing learning competitions at her school.

The fact that educational perspectives position educators and students to see and act in the world in different ways precludes the possibility of educators picking and choosing among those perspectives in order to build a supermodel of a literacy program "that works." Attempts to establish such eclectic programs typically arise from advocates of psychological or cultural literacy education who recognize that their traditional control over elementary and secondary schooling is beginning to slip. They begin with caricatures of naturalistic and critical perspectives as being either without worthwhile content and teaching or too political and without skills. From these caricatures, they pluck activities—individual choices over topics for reading and writing, collaboration, and the "real world," popular focus—and place them within the "skills first" or "best of the past" focus of their own approach. Armed with these apparent concessions to the advocates of other perspectives, these eclectic educators proclaim their programs to be "what works" without actually compromising any of their basic tenets but completely compromising naturalistic and critical assumptions.

"What works" arguments appear compelling at first glance because they seem to be a compromise of the old with the new—a "balanced" approach to schooling and literacy education among what are often hotly debated positions. Picking the best from each perspective appeals to Americans' pragmatic, down-to-earth, and problem-solving approach to life. This blending makes our choices seem easy—we can have everything. However, pragmatism is based on an analysis of the possible and probable consequences of any course of action before it is undertaken to determine if that course is in line with our goals—our answers to the question of how we wish to live together. Educators who suggest a "what works" literacy program should be asked to explain how their blended variety accommodates the different perspectives' answers to that question. The simple answer is that they do not.

Advocates of each perspective typically parrot the old Superman (the one before D. C. Comics killed and resurrected him) to claim that they alone are working toward "truth, justice, and the American way." However when pressed, advocates of each perspective have quite different goals for school and life. Advocates of "what works" approaches still establish arbitrary competitions to determine who shall benefit from schooling and who shall not. While they claim that merit is the only thing that will be rewarded through a "what works" curriculum, they privilege some students over others by selecting certain skills and content as the agreed-upon curricula that is of most value. Within "what works" programs, the appropriated elements of naturalistic and critical discourses are secondary to the primary goal of transmission of skills and/or content of the psychological and cultural literacy. Try as they might to be fair, "what works" advocates end up rewarding students whose backgrounds and experiences seem closest to their own and labeling students with different backgrounds and experiences as "deficient," "at risk," even "pathological."

Advocates of "what works" curricula define *truth* as their own position, *justice* as the outcome of biased learning competitions ("Let the market decide"), and the *American way* as one that promotes the self-interests of powerful social groups and those who wish to become powerful. Coopting aspects of naturalistic or critical perspectives will not change the direction of a psychological or cultural literacy programs. Advocates of "what works" should be asked, works for what and for whom?

To leave learning competitions and intolerance of difference behind, educators must move beyond psychological or cultural literacy programs to establish naturalistic and critical perspectives. Naturalistic educational programs dispense with competitions and embrace difference—at least at the personal level. It will, however, leave students to contemplate the competitive nature of the world. If we acknowledge the savage inequalities in schools and our lives, our point is to engage the world actively in order to change it. For that, we need leaders and critical literacy education.

Chapter 6

Developing Critical Literacy Education

Last summer was so hot that we fled to the movies at every opportunity to enjoy an air-conditioned two-hour vacation. We watched talking animals make their way home over hundreds of miles; a boy pitch for the Chicago Cubs because the tendons in his broken arm healed improperly; a young girl grow a new life for herself, her relations, and friends; and the story of a boy and a whale's return to family life. This last film, *Free Willy* (1993, Warner), captured our attention and that of many families because it seemed to speak to participation in civic life in ways seldom seen on big or small screens. First, Tim-Pat, Laura, and I went to see it when Kathleen was away, and then as the heat wave continued, we saw it again as a family.

Free Willy offered a 1990s twist on the familiar children's theme of a troubled youth who comes to understand herself and others through a relationship with an animal. There was *Lassie* and *Black Beauty* before my time and *Ol' Yeller* from my childhood. *Free Willy* is filled with references to contemporary problems—the environment, homeless children, and adult male roles in families. The film's plot seems simple and is emotional. An orca whale is captured and sold to the Northwest Adventure Park as Willy, the performing whale. Jesse, an abandoned child who has escaped from a juvenile home, is caught while vandalizing Willy's holding tank and is sentenced to repair the damage and to live as a foster child with Glen Greenwood, a garage owner, and his wife, Annie, a teacher.

As Jesse works around Willy, they develop a relationship that enables Jesse to train Willy to perform tricks despite Willy's troubled relationship with his female professional trainer, Raye, and the Park's Native American handyman, Randolph. Jesse rapidly develops a sense of belonging with Randolph and Raye around the care of Willy. However, he remains distant from his foster parents because he believes that his mother will return for him "after she gets a few things worked out." Jesse's sense of belonging quickly disintegrates when Willy refuses to perform his tricks before a crowd that his owner has promoted at great expense. Trying to recoup his money, the owner, Dial, decides to cause an accident to the holding tank that will kill Willy and bring an insurance settlement. Jesse uncovers this plot, discovers that Willy's family awaits him in the bay just outside the park, and organizes a plan to free Willy, all during his attempt to run away from his foster parents and his failure as an animal trainer.

In the end, Jesse, Randolph, and Raye need Jesse's foster father's help to free Willy against impossible odds. It takes Randolph's spiritualism and Jesse's love to will Willy over a twenty-foot-high channel barrier in order for Willy to again swim with his family. Because of Glen's efforts, Jesse realizes that he has found his own family also. Fade to black with Michael Jackson singing "Will You Be There?" based on the tune that Jesse played on his harmonica to communicate with Willy.

The second time through the film, both Laura and Tim-Pat had questions about it. Tim-Pat wanted to know how the filmmakers were able to get Willy to do all the stunts. From a visit to the Baltimore National Aquarium, he remembered that the trainers had explicitly stated that the tricks the dolphins and seals performed were actually extensions of the animals' natural motions. Laura confirmed this information in Marguerite Henry's *White Stallion of Lipizza* (1994, Macmillan), a story about the training of Lipizzaner horses. But in the film, Willy sang to his unseen family, rode on an exposed trailer, and displayed a temper, all of which Tim-Pat considered to be unnatural behaviors for a whale. In *People* magazine of all places, we found that the unnatural stunts were done by an "animatronic" whale, and that Keiko, who played Willy in the film, is not free at all and is an animal performer at a Mexican amusement park. Tim-Pat thought the former explained how a whale could jump twenty feet over Jesse's head, and the latter, he complained, "is not fair."

Tim-Pat's first question opened a floodgate of concerns that our children had as they used *Free Willy* to make better sense of their own lives and the world around them. For example, Laura wanted to know why the women, Raye and Annie, had such small parts, why people catch whales, and how children can live on the street. Tim-Pat wanted to know how Jesse and his friends could get into so much trouble without going to jail, why Randolph wore a baseball cap for most of the movie but put on a headband during the climax, and finally why Jesse didn't want to play baseball with Glen. Kathleen and I hoped they would explore their too-easy stance on freeing confined animals, the paradox of Jesse's attempt to participate in the exploitation of Willy, and the underlying theme of "normal" American family values.

Laura is particularly sensitive to the lack of women and girls with significant roles in children's films. She complains frequently that there are few films for young girls. Disney seems to make live-action films for boys and animated features for girls. The best female role of the summer from Disney, she thought, was a cat with Sally Fields' voice. The cat was on the screen as often as any other character, said as much as other characters, and appeared to be smart and courageous. In contrast, Annie and Raye, while supportive, nurturing, and consistent, were also submissive, dependent, and slow to act. They are a far cry from the women she studies at school: Harriett Tubman, Lucretia Mott, or Rosa Parks. Or the ones in the biographies that her grandmother sends her: Susan B. Anthony, Elizabeth Cady Stanton, or Lucy Stone. Nor are they like her mother, her aunt, or her grandmother.

The issue of catching whales is brought into high relief on the videotape version of *Free Willy*. Before the film begins, Michael Jackson performs the theme song with quick cuts to film footage of whales swimming in the ocean. At the end of the song, an advertisement for Earth Island Institute asks viewers to "adopt an orca" by calling an 800 number and sending twenty-five dollars (shipping and handling included). This last bit of information prompted Tim-Pat to ask where we would keep our adopted whale. Just before this request leaves the screen, the sponsor of the Earth Island Institute is revealed. It's Bumble Bee Tuna Seafood, Inc. Much of this is too subtle for children to catch. Michael Jackson has a multi-million dollar contract with Sony Corporation, a Japanese conglomerate, which at the moment of this writing owns Warner Brothers, a fleet of fishing vessels, and Bumble Bee Tuna among many other things. Japan is one of the few countries that refused to sign the international treaty to ban whaling. Laura did notice the Bumble Bee Tuna sponsor and remembered that dolphins get caught in tuna nets and drown. She learned this while reading magazines and books about mammals while she was in first grade. Laura wondered, "Why would a tuna company want to protect whales? It's advertising, isn't it, Dad?"

The screenwriter and director of *Free Willy* take every opportunity to distinguish Willy's owner, Dial, and his assistant from the rest of the cast. Everyone is slim and handsome except for Dial's henchman, who cooks up the insurance scheme. The shifty-eyed Dial originally purchased Willy to attract customers to his adventure park. However, Willy was an adolescent when he was captured and Raye couldn't break through Willy's "attitude" in order to turn him into a moneymaker. Dial paid five-thousand-dollar premiums for a one-million-dollar insurance policy to protect his investment. After every disappointment, Dial exclaims, "I hate that whale!" But Dial did not have the proper facilities to accommodate Willy in the first place. Raye makes the definitive statement about Dial when she explains to Jesse that "Dial thinks he can treat a wild animal like a commodity." During our last viewing, Tim-Pat asked me at this point in the film, "What's a commodity?" When I stopped the videotape to explain that a commodity is something for sale, Tim-Pat quoted a section of the movie to show that he understood. "Oh, it's like when Dial says 'The Willy show! It will make money. And that, my friend, is what we're all about. This could be big. This could be real big.'"

The profit motive is a confusing issue for Laura and Tim-Pat. They realize that Dial was greedy—he bought poor food for Willy, wouldn't build the appropriate holding tank, and thought of Willy as only a commodity. However, they wondered about all of the animal shows that they have watched at zoos, aquariums, and amusement parks, and in films and on television. Were those animals treated as commodities? Moreover, do the families in our neighborhood who breed dogs treat the puppies as commodities? And if treating animals as commodities is bad, why did Raye, Randolph, and Jesse eagerly participate in making the wild orca into "Willy"? If you love or respect the animate commodity, does that make it proper? *Free Willy* identifies some interesting intersections between economics and ethics that Tim-Pat and Laura found challenging to their own everyday behavior as well as the business world.

Race becomes an issue in *Free Willy* on two occasions. Tim-Pat's question about the cap and headband points to the running theme of Native American spiritualism in the film. Early in the story, Randolph tells Jesse a Haida legend about the creation of the orca and its rescue of an early chief of his people. When it comes time to free Willy, Randolph remembers the legend and is prepared to return the favor. His memory and decision are symbolized by his removal of his baseball cap—a part of the unofficial uniform of the American working class—and its replacement with a headband. Although Tim-Pat was unable to articulate this culture switch, he recognized that something important had happened in that film detail. As we discussed possible rationales for including the legend and culture switching, Laura invoked the controversy about the illustrations in the picture book *Brother Eagle, Sister Sky*, (1991, Dial) which homogenized different Native American cultures into one. Laura was suspicious of how accurately the Native American markers were used in the film.

The second explicit reference to race was Randolph's remark that Jesse was "one lucky white boy" when Willy saved his life after he fell, hit his head, and rolled into the holding tank while unconscious. Because of Willy's early reputation at the park, Randolph thought Jesse was fortunate not to have been eaten. The term *white boy* made color a natural point for discussion. Only three characters in the film were played by people of color: Dwight, Jesse's juvenile caseworker, is African American; a fishmonger from whom Jesse stole and bought fish for Willy is Asian American; and Randolph is Native American. Only Dwight and Randolph had prominent parts, and only Randolph had to be a person of color because Dwight's role did not identify him as an African American in the same way that Randolph's identified him as a Native American. Although two is better than none I guess, the lack of other characters of color distorts some of the issues that the film attempts to explore.

For example, contrary to published demographic statistics, *Free Willy* has an all-white band of homeless, runaways, and street kids at the beginning of the film when Jesse is on his own. They panhandle, steal leftover food from restaurant tables, and spray paint walls. Perhaps these are antisocial behaviors, but certainly they are not serious crimes. They appear to live by their wits. After Jesse is caught and tucked safely at Glen and Annie's home, the band reappears periodically as a gang to tempt Jesse back to street life. On the first occasion, the gang is multiracial, and their white leader, Perry, asks Jesse to join them as lookouts for adults who perform simple robberies. Later when Perry returns with a black eye, he invites Jesse to accompany him and his adult mentor to Venice, California, apparently to increase the profitability of their "business." That's where Jesse's headed when he interrupts Dial's plot to kill Willy. After Jesse left the street, race is portrayed as a menace to society.

Laura's question about children's lives on the street and Tim-Pat's concern about kids getting into trouble come together in a racial analysis of the street kids. We consulted *The State of America's Children* (by the Children's Defense Fund) to determine who is more likely to be homeless or on the street in America. Over 25 percent of Americans live below the poverty line, and the poverty rate has been growing over the last fifteen years. Children under the age of six comprise the fastest growing percentage of the poor. Out of 100 poor children in America, 28 live in suburban areas, 27 in rural areas, and 45 in cities; 41 are European American, 35 are African American, 21 are Latino, and 3 are Asian American, Pacific Islander, Native American, or Alaska Native. It's unlikely that homeless and street children would all be white as *Free Willy* portrays them. If the filmmakers hoped to explore the issue of caring for poor American children, they missed an opportunity to help viewers recognize and acknowledge just who those children are likely to be.

Even after repeated escapes from juvenile homes and conflicts with the police, Dwight is able to spare Jesse a sentence to the detention center, the "juvenile jail." He tells Jesse that because he is young, he'll get some chances. Tim-Pat recognized that Jesse's offenses warranted a greater response than a chance to train a whale and to live in a house with a 180-degree panoramic view of the ocean from your bedroom. He wanted to know if Jesse's reprieve had anything to do with the Jim Crow laws that he'd heard about at school and when his sister read Rosa Parks's autobiography, *My Story* (1993, Dial), aloud at home. "You know, like when Rosa Parks got arrested because she wouldn't stand up for a white man on the bus in Birmingham, Alabama. It's a double standard." I took this comment to mean that he believed that Jesse's preferential treatment had more to do with the color of his skin than his age.

The conflict over whether Jesse will play baseball with Glen captures the film's attempt to affirm normal American values. After all, except for moms and apple pie, what's more stereotypically American than baseball? Jesse repeatedly refuses to play catch or to worship the baseball Glen offers him as a welcoming present. Tim-Pat, who was poised to begin a career as a T-ball "star," couldn't understand why Jesse won't engage in "having a catch." I asked him what he thought it meant to play ball with Glen from Jesse's point of view. "Well, he'd have to like Glen." "Does he like Glen?" "He can't and still love his mother. Don't you remember you can't have two loves? That's why Glen said he had to sell his red car when he married Annie." There's the rub for Jesse. Jesse stands outside of a two-parent family tradition because he holds onto the dream that his impoverished mother will return after a six-year absence. To break Jesse's grip on this dream, Dwight and Glen disparage Jesse's mother. "She just dropped you off and drove away. She didn't even look back. What kind of a mother is that?" It's the kind that makes Jesse an abnormal American—poor and from a single-parent home. Ironically but not surprisingly, Jesse's biological father is never mentioned in the film. To play ball with Glen, then, would require Jesse to renounce his mother. Everyone in the film seems just as intent on making Jesse normal by bringing him into a financially secure, two-parent family as they are on freeing Willy. Of course, they are "successful" in both endeavors. As Jesse confesses, "Some mother! She couldn't even take care of herself, let alone me." When Raye tells Jesse, "Willy's a case, a very special case," Jesse replies, "So, who isn't?" Apparently, we all need fixing.

When asked, Tim-Pat and Laura thought *Free Willy* was about saving whales and "maybe the environment, too. You know, the rainforest and stuff." Among their supporting evidence was the advertisement to adopt an orca. As we talked about this message, Tim-Pat asked about raising money to adopt "lots" of orcas. Laura explained that she had written a one-minute television spot for rainforests as a persuasive writing assignment at school. They both like the idea of being involved in saving the planet. However, this is just one type of action available to them, and we discussed how they could help personally to save the environment. They talked about turning the water and lights off promptly when not in use. Laura suggested that our family could drive our car less. Tim-Pat thought we could pick up trash.

Although these solutions are useful, they do not seem to translate *Free Willy's* message directly to our lives. If Willy represents the environment, then it is greed that is a threat to our world and national and local environments. To protect the local environment against greed means that we must recognize the hazards that are much closer to our home in Pennsylvania than whales and the Brazilian rainforest and participate actively in local civic life. That is, we must be aware and act upon the federal Superfund cleanup of Spring Creek, pollution that turned Fisherman's Paradise into a ghost town even on the opening day of fishing season, the *Giardia* problems in the drinking water of a nearby town, or local dairy farmers' addition of hormones to their cows' feed to increase their milk yield. Moreover, we must explore why the local paper, the *Centre Daily Times*, seems to neglect these and other environmental issues in our area. Our discussion about activism against greed reminded Tim-Pat of another movie, *Newsies* (1992, Touchstone), a film that Disney released about the New York City paperboy strike at the turn of the century. As a family we decided to refuse to stand by silently while our local environment is held captive to profits.

At first glance, *Free Willy* may not seem to be a text worthy of prolonged extensive study. It's just a kid's movie. And for some children, it may not be worthy. But for Tim-Pat and Laura, *Free Willy* is an important text, one which invited many readings. They saw it twice in the theater when there were other films from which to choose; they talked about it often; they invoked scenes and dialogue from it during discussions of apparently unrelated topics as metaphors or corroborating evidence for their opinion; and they agreed eagerly to reconsider it slowly using a VCR. Because this bit of popular culture proved important to Tim-Pat and Laura at this time, it became a worthy curricular text for our critical literacy education.

Critical literacy alters the definition, content, and processes of traditional literacy lessons. As I described in chapter 5, rather than a single collection of cognitive skills to reproduce meanings from or through print, critical literacy becomes the ability to use multiple texts, including all symbol systems and expressions of disparate points of view, to make sense of one's life and the world in a particular context. Literacy, like all other social relations, is influenced by the social situation in which it is used. That is, reading to assemble your bicycle with your children watching is different than writing poetry to a loved one, which in turn is different than reading and writing many texts during an IRS audit. Each situation presents unique opportunities and constraints for our literacy. However, traditional school literacy is only appropriate in traditional schools. In fact, individuals and groups must overcome their school lessons in order to meet the varied literacy demands of their daily life.

The literacy that surrounded our consideration of *Free Willy* demonstrates ways in which Tim-Pat, Laura, and I could each contribute actively and constructively to our individual and collective understanding of ourselves and the world. Tim-Pat, who was just beginning to use print, read his own experience, lectures he's heard at museums, and other movies to interpret this film. The sophistication of his literacies is shown in his attention to detail and wonder about characters' intentions and is captured in his critique of Hollywood: "I can't wait 'til they catch Willy again, so we can see *Willy 2!*" Laura uses many texts (films, songs, and books) to test the author's and directors' messages and intentions in *Free Willy*. While her print literacy is more conventional than Tim-Pat's, it does not overshadow or minimize his other literacies. Print literacy gives her more options, but it does not necessarily make her reading of *Free Willy* superior to Tim-Pat's. Both Tim-Pat and Laura expect all texts and all their literacies to make sense, but they realize as Laura states, "One version [text] doesn't tell the whole story, Dad. Think about *Beauty and the Beast*. All the books and the movie are different."

The content and processes of critical literacy education stem directly from this definition of literacy. The content becomes the participants' lives in all their transdisciplinary and cross-aged splendor. Teachers' and students' lives, of course, must be placed in their immediate and historical contexts to be comprehensible. This requires a careful distinction to be made between the creation of physical and social reality. The latter is the result of past and present human intentions and actions—expressions of power—which can be understood through the participants' efforts to see whose interests are truly served and perhaps changed by thoughtful collective acts of those who listen to the disparate voices seeking more just and equitable civic life for all of us.

For example, Laura and Tim-Pat used *Free Willy* to consider the environment and economics and race, gender, and class relations. Their apparently simple questions led to sustained, complex discussions that cut across the boundaries of school disciplines in ways that required both breadth and depth of knowledge. While they were trying to understand what transpires in the film, they were working on how they will live in their world. How does greed effect them? Do they use symbols to show their cultural background? What is their relationship to their father? These are not random thoughts on their parts; they are the complexities of their lives with which they must deal on a daily basis. Their questions are not inconsequential, childlike, or beside the point of what every American should know. Rather, they are central concerns for children, and for all of our lives. I learned about myself and others by listening to and discussing these issues with Tim-Pat and Laura. Uncovering the symbolism of Randolph's headband required sophisticated, mutual scaffolding of what we collectively know about issues of importance in anthropology, psychology, and art. While I may know more about these subjects than either Tim-Pat or Laura, I must admit that I did not notice the baseball cap for headband switch until Tim-Pat mentioned it and Laura was the one who remembered that the headband made Randolph look like the rescued chief in the Haida legend. Together, we made our anthropological hypothesis about their connections, which helped us understand the film in a different way.

Tim-Pat, Laura, and I discussed the concerns and interests that accompanied our repeated viewing of *Free Willy*. Each of us was able to pose and pursue questions that helped us come to grips with the ideas behind the film and how those ideas fit into our lives. We did not agree on every point and some of our hypotheses may be unique to our discussion and analyses because of the way we raised our questions and attempted our answers. However, each hypothesis was based on careful dialogue in which three earnest learners worked to make sense of this text within the context of what we know about the world. Because of our efforts, we now know considerably more about that world and about ourselves than we did when we started.

The methods we used to initiate, maintain, and conclude our analysis of *Free Willy* present a glimpse at the processes of critical literacy education: a question-centered approach, an extended sense of dialogue, and activism based on that new knowledge. Our study of *Free Willy* began with Tim-Pat's question about the training of the whale in the film. As we pursued this question—actually we stumbled across an answer while waiting in line at the grocery store that displayed *People* on its checkout counter—other questions about the film arose. Our interest in *Free Willy* was always driven by our own questions, although at times our pursuit of answers meant that we had to address other questions as partial responses to our originals. In the end, we posed some larger questions that we will be addressing for the rest of our lives: Why do people treat other people, animals, and the enviroment as commodities? What makes a family? Why are there poor people?

Because we worked from our own questions according to our own criteria for good answers, we challenged theories of learning that suggest that information must be transmitted from teachers and texts to students according to fixed schedules and plans. Our efforts taught us that the world can be approached as an object to be understood and known by our own efforts. The world is largely knowable—it is not magic—although it is not necessarily known by simply swallowing all that we are told because we are only told parts of "the story" through the media, institutions, and structures of everyday life. That is why we used our literacies to search through multiple texts in order to address what is and is not told to us in *Free Willy*. While expert opinion (as from museum spokespeople) was valuable in these efforts, we looked also for experts with varying points of view (as from the Children's Defense Fund) in order to check our facts. Moreover, we sought voices that aren't usually recognized as experts by official sources (children's fiction authors, people of color, and women) to fill in the silences in the texts. Finally, we called upon our own expertise to analyze and evaluate the film and its ideas.

A second process within critical literacy education is the use of dialogue as the primary way to address the questions we posed. In this context, dialogue is more than conversation, and it cannot be scripted to lead toward some predetermined end. Rather dialogues are genuine, open exchanges among students and teachers that are situated in their language, culture, and questions and are centered on helping all to illuminate and eventually to act on their realities. These exchanges require more than talk while sitting around a table. They are not excuses for teachers, parents, or anyone else to lecture while all others sit and listen. Dialogues must be informed by texts and data that participants gather and bring to the exchanges. Through the actions necessary to gather that information and the information itself, participants help each other to clarify their thoughts and positions by probing contradictions and inconsistencies. Others who bring different experiences, discourses, and intentions to the exchange can push comfortable hypotheses and conclusions in helpful ways. For example, when Tim-Pat, Laura, and I became satisfied with our condemnation of Dial's relationship with Willy, one question from Kathleen forced us to acknowledge our own involvement in treating animals as commodities. Dialogue then afforded us the opportunity to express our thoughts, but it also required us to be responsible for them.

Our dialogue was not conducted among equals. I am one of Laura's and Tim-Pat's parents with all the power and responsibility vested in that role. I cannot and should not renounce that power and responsibility to facilitate my own or their learning. Teachers cannot and should not negate the power and responsibility they hold in their classrooms and schools in order to engage in dialogue with their students. However, we can join genuine and open dialogues in homes and schools if we are willing to admit that we and our students are all people, and that as people, we are incomplete and contradictory in both our beliefs and actions. As parents and teachers, we do not know and do not need to know everything to retain our authority. In fact, we become better parents and teachers, I think, if we acknowledge our lack of encyclopedic knowledge of the world and all that's in it and demonstrate our desire and ability to learn. Moreover, we become better dialogue partners when we also express our confidence that all others can become our teachers as we teach them.

Dialogue will continue the contemplative nature of traditional literacy education unless it is coupled with activism based on the new knowledge participants produce. It is not enough to entertain and inform ourselves through literacy, particularly when we find the world and ourselves lacking. We must act—it is our civic responsibility to act according to our informed convictions in order to find more just and equitable ways to live together. In response to *Free Willy*, Tim-Pat, Laura, and I decided to follow the advice from a bumper sticker we've seen—think globally, but act locally. Initially, we've decided to regulate our use of energy and resources—

Tim-Pat will remember to turn off the lights when he leaves a room, Laura will not waste so much paper, and I will carry my bicycle out of the basement and ride it to work. Although these acts may not change the world, they do connect our lives with those of others and society. Beyond these personal acts we joined the boycott of dairy farmers and dairy corporations that use hormonal additives and we circulated petitions and attended rallies for the Clear Water Initiative in Pennsylvania. After careful study, we decided to join Greenpeace, an effective and activist environmental organization. We're still undecided about whether we will attend performing animal shows anymore.

Since our dialogue about *Free Willy* considered more than the environment, we've decided to act upon our new knowledge about gender biases, greed, poverty, double standards in laws and regulations, sensitivity to culture and race, and expanding family values. At this point, most of our actions involve confronting our biases about differences. For example, Tim-Pat and I are working to become more familiar with girls' and women's ways of knowing and acting so that we can confront our tendencies to turn all social relations into competitions. We are a family of writers, and so we write letters to editors, petitions, poetry, short stories, articles, and books that identify contradictions within these matters in order to join others in their work to diminish social biases and their consequences.

In order to act, we must believe that our actions could make a difference in our own and others' lives. If we didn't hold this belief, why would we bother to act at all? In part, this belief is an expected outcome of asking and attempting to answer our own questions. A question-centered approach to education breeds active learners. But to participate actively in civic life, we must become more than active learners. We must approach the social world as a created, transformable reality that was put in place and is maintained according to human interests. If the social world is a human artifact, then it is changeable through the acts of other human beings. This concept is not too abstract for children to comprehend. Even *Free Willy* imparts this message. Moreover, seeking to make a difference through your actions presupposes that you have considered the possibility of making new social realities. That is, your intent to act means that you are willing to take the next step after asking why things are the way they are to consider what those things should become.

The transformation of active learners to active participants in civic life requires formal demonstrations. Unfortunately, most children lack access to people who model these transformations in any way beyond voting. And less than 50 percent of eligible adults even bother to do that. Our family has found recent children's books and music as well as literature and music not typically considered to be for children to provide invaluable texts to fill this void. Along with the biographies of Mother Jones, Frederick Douglas, César Chávez, Rachel Carson, and Mary Bethune Cookman are songs about Harriett Tubman, Joe Hill, Lucretia Mott, and Stephen Biko. Kathleen and I wonder what the outcome will be of Tim-Pat and Laura learning to sing "Lifeline" (Holly Near's and Ronnie Gilbert's song about the underground railroad), "Are My Hands Clean?" (Sweet Honey in the Rock's song about the exploitation of third-world workers by multinational clothing corporations), "Bourgeoisie Blues" (Leadbelly's song about segregation in the nation's capital), or "Deportee" (Woody Guthrie's song about illegal migrant workers) rather than "The Marine Hymn" or "As the Caissons Go Rolling Along" as we did when we were their age.

There are books about channeling resistance through art (such as *Tar Beach* by Faith Ringgold, 1994, Crown Books), personal responsibility (such as *We Are All in the Dumps with Jack and Guy* by Maurice Sendak, 1993, Harper Collins), the legal system (such as *Morning Star, Black Sun* by Brent Ashabranner, 1992, Putnam) or collective demonstration (such as *Trouble at the Mines* by Doreen Rappaport, 1987, Bantam-Skylark). *Sami and the Time of the Troubles* (by Florence Heide and Judith Gilliland, 1992, Clarion Books) describes life for children in Beirut during the struggle over Lebanon, including the spontaneous "Day of the Children" protest of the pro-longed fighting. And there are accounts of what happens when the oppressed are frustrated with inaction and lose hope for change through peaceful means, such as: *My Brother, Sam, Is Dead* (by James and Lincoln Colliers, 1994, MacMillan, a book about the beginning of the American Revolution), *John Brown: One Man Against Slavery* (by Gwen Everett, 1993, Rizzoli), *The Haymarket Riot* (by Charnan Simon, 1988, Children's), *Farmer Duck* (by Martin Waddell, 1992, Candlewick, an allegory about the violent overthrow of oppressors), and *Smoky Nights* (by Eve Bunting, 1994, Harcourt Brace, a picture book about children during the recent uprising in Los Angeles after the first Rodney King verdict).

All these texts provide historical and current alternatives available to activists who intend to make a difference. Like other texts, they are not beyond reproach and should be ana-lyzed in the same way that Laura, Tim-Pat, and I considered *Free Willy*. Moreover, reading and listening are prerequisites but not substitutes for thoughtful activism based on careful analyses of unjust and inequitable social practices. With the knowledge that the world is knowable, that current injustices are the result of unequal power relations of the past and present, and that we have the capabilities, the right, and the responsibility to act, parents, children, students, and teachers are prepared to use a question-centered approach, dialogue, and activism in order to become more active participants in the civic life of their neighborhoods, their communities, and the larger world.

Of course, we should be prepared when our children take us at our word and act. For example, when Tim-Pat was three, he responded to my attempts to wring the names of his friends who perpetuated some heinous crime against humanity with a rousing chorus from Woody Guthrie's "Union Maids": "You can't scare me, I'm stickin' to the union 'til the day I die!"

Chapter 7

Talking Back to Critics

*T*here I was, sitting on a dais with three other speakers, waiting for my turn to stand behind the podium to make a short speech. I supposed that this was to be a bit of an advertisement for my workshop on critical literacy education at a teachers' conference the next day in the same building. It was Thursday night and the audience was comprised of two hundred or so teachers, school administrators, and parents, all of whom had put in a full day of work before arriving. I had flown across the country to be there, and it was three hours later in my biorhythms than on the clock in the room. I was scheduled to speak last and was simultaneously concerned and happy about it. I was worried about how drowsy the audience and I would be when my opportunity to speak came and about whether the other speakers would "run long" and usurp my time. But I also kidded myself that the conference schedulers had saved the best for last.

The first speaker, a noted educational psychologist, presented fascinating statistics and research about illiteracy in America. She worried about the unscientific speculation that other so-called "experts" offered for what should happen in schools, particularly urban schools. This had a familiar ring to it for me. She remarked that because children come from homes that no longer prepare them for literacy learning at school, schooling should begin for three- and four-year-olds and their parents. Looking to her left where I sat with another speaker, the educational psychologist suggested that contrary to popular belief, children will not learn to read by themselves. Rather they must be taught "the code," and she had the research to prove it.

The woman sitting next to me spoke next. She seemed a bit flustered at first, apparently because she took personally what had just been said. After two minutes of her allotted ten, she put her notes aside and presented an eloquent extemporaneous speech on how people—all people—learn and use language. Moreover, she declared that written language was indeed language, and was therefore learned and used like oral language. She charged that teaching the code had been tried and had failed in school for that very reason. Her examples were drawn from studies conducted in inner-city homes and schools, which showed that parents and siblings provided many more opportunities for children to talk, read, and write —that is, to learn and use oral and written language—than did classrooms that featured direct language teaching. And she had the research to prove it. This was an exciting exchange but just before she returned to her seat she made a closing remark that other so-called experts on urban literacy were advocating content and methods that would rob children of their childhood. I could swear she nodded toward me as she said that.

I was becoming uncomfortable about my position in the speaking order, but at least I was no longer concerned about staying alert. The third speaker was from the Eagle Forum, a national organization headed by Phyllis Schlafly, which has taken public stands against women's rights, affirmative action, sex education, and free speech in student newspapers, as well as affirming many other conservative positions. She began with a prayer for our schools and our school children—that they may be saved from New Age liberals, the politically correct, homosexuals, and the unpatriotic. Halfway into a talk that supported explicit teaching of phonics, grammar, and family values as they had been taught in the *McGuffey Readers* of the nineteenth century, she stopped, turned toward me, and said, "I've read Professor Shannon's work, and he's not only politically correct, he's not a patriot." I'm not certain what she said after that because my mind went blank. To be honest, I'm not just slow afoot.

When it came my turn to speak, I was not sure what to do, but I was convinced that I was not really paranoid because people really were after me. I'd like to report that I dazzled the audience and was as brilliant as the second speaker had been. I wish I could have stood and delivered a rousing defense of myself, my work, and critical literacy education. But I did not. I had been labeled unscientific, doctrinaire, and unpatriotic in less that thirty minutes and I sincerely wished I had missed my flight to the conference that afternoon. I had heard that some consider my work unscientific before and some have described my position as doctrinaire. But this was the first time I'd been called unpatriotic (to my face, anyway). I couldn't help wondering if perhaps the last speaker was correct. I thought maybe I am unpatriotic. At that time, I handled the situation with humor. I joked that I was happy to be there, and pointing to my suit and tie I remarked that my mother was incorrect when she said, "Pat, if you don't know anything, dress nicely and no one will care." I smiled and said that it was nice to have so many readers of my work. By the end of my ten minutes, the audience wondered why the others had been so nasty to poor little me. If I had it to do again though, this is what I would say.

I am a patriot. I am personally committed to making the United States honest and just in all its acts—just as I am committed to making my acts honest and just with others. As a patriot, I am vigorous in celebrating the good qualities and deeds of Americans and our culture as we seek peace, freedom, and self-determined social justice. Americans are at our best when we act unself-consciously moral toward others, hoping to share with them what we enjoy for no other reason than that they too are human beings who, if you make a semantic substitution in our most valued text, are all equal with certain inalienable rights.

As a patriot, I am just as vigorous in criticizing and urging corrections of my country's failures, omissions, and wrongs—

just as I am self-critical and expect others to criticize me for the same. I act on these celebrations and criticisms with my pen, with my time and strength, and with my possessions. I struggle actively for a government and a set of institutions that increase the possibility of our realizing peace, freedom, and justice. This struggle for better government is the patriotic thing to do because patriots, just like me, have made a difference in how Americans live today.

You must remember that when this country started, people of African descent were considered only three-fifths human, that women had few property rights and no right to vote, and that Native Americans had no right to live at all. At different times, slavery was an accepted practice, supported by the government, defended by the military, and at the center of the political spectrum; denial of women's rights to vote was accepted, supported, defended and at the political center; and leaving workers without pensions, medical care, or the right to organize was accepted, supported, defended, and at the political center. Unchecked monopolies, exploitation of the environment, and apartheid in schools and public life were at the political center. All of these failures, omissions, and wrongs were finally addressed only after patriots seeking peace, freedom, and justice for all human beings were able to step out of the truly political corrective behavior of conservative self-interest and demonstrate these acts and laws to be intolerable, morally indefensible, and antidemocratic.

Of course, these words and facts can be distorted so that peace becomes the justification for the massacre of nonwhite civilians, including women and children in Grenada, Panama, Iraq, and Somalia, so that freedom becomes the right to go without needed health care or to own a handgun, so that justice is something that can be purchased, and patriotism is something you can tie up in a yellow ribbon. These distortions of truth have been the politically correct positions of the 1980s and 1990s according to the government, media, business, and religious right, and they show us that language is indeed political and at the center of politics.

What is missed when critical education is labeled politically correct or unpatriotic is an important distinction between politicized and political education. A politicized education indoctrinates students toward a specific political agenda. It's an education where what can be taught, who can teach it, and how and where it can be taught to whom is decided with little regard for truth beyond platitudes and for evidence beyond hearsay. A political education, on the other hand, aims to teach students how to think and act in ways that cultivate the capacity for judgment essential for active participation in civic life. Without setting the content beforehand and without settling on a single definition of thinking, political education prepares participants to exercise power and responsibility of a democratic citizenry. A political, as distinct from a politicized, education encourages participants to become patriotic in order to challenge those with political and cultural power as well as to honor the critical traditions within the United States that make such critiques possible and appropriate.

This is the tension—to critique while celebrating and to celebrate while critiquing—that is missing from concerns that the Eagle Forum and conservative Christian fundamentalists express about public schooling and naturalistic and critical perspectives. Although they are by no means a single voice, these groups propose a politicized education based on their reading of the Bible and their corresponding interpretation of how society should serve God. Citizens for Excellence in Education, the American Family Association, the Christian Coalition, the Eagle Forum, Focus on the Family, and the Traditional Values Coalition all use various tactics to ensure that school curricula, materials, instruction, and policy correspond with strict, literal translation of the church doctrines. In their struggles against Satan, they oppose magic-based fantasy, positive references to non-Christian religions, multiculturalism, curriculum integration, teaching evolution, sex education, cooperative learning, environmental education, and even aerobics in gym classes.

Some believe that educators are in effect conspiring, as Mel and Norma Gabler state in their book *What Are They Teaching Our Children?* (1985, Victor), "to tear down traditional faith, even if it means permitting the occult to enter the classroom. They are skilled at pouring their anti-God dogmas into the void." In *The Inspirational Writings of Pat Robertson* (1989, Arrowood), the then-presidential candidate states, "The humanism that is being taught in our schools, media, and intellectual circles will ultimately lead people to the Anti-Christ, because he will be the consummate figure of humanism." What makes this conspiracy unpatriotic to these conservative Christians is that the United States is a "Christian nation." The Reverend Jerry Falwell, founder of the now-bankrupt Moral Majority, reports that

> America was founded by Godly men who had in mind establishing a republic not only Christian in nature, but a republic designed to propagate the Gospel worldwide. (as quoted in *The Fundamentalist Phenomenon*, 1990, Eerdmans)

To "return" schools to their religious roots, Robert Simonds, president and founder of Citizens for Excellence in Education (CEE) calls for Christians to "get organized for battle because this *is* a spiritual battle (*Educational Leadership*, 1994, 12–15)." The CEE and other conservative Christian fundamentalist groups recommend that parents volunteer in schools and for curriculum development committees, for district and state textbook selection panels, and for personnel review boards. They tap a national network of organizations to inform parents about issues and "threats to Christian values" that are proposed or are being implemented in school districts across the country. In this sense, the literature among these Christian groups is noticeably similar. According to Simonds, his organization has "no trouble getting help for their cause from Excel [a coalition of CEOs and corporations] and other corporate-financed groups."

CEE membership has grown remarkably over the last decade from 50 to 210,000 members and has distributed thousands of Public School Awareness Committee kits stating: "Yes, every public school is actually teaching the doctrines of an atheist ideology.... This is illegal and must be stopped. Here is how." The kit goes on to describe techniques that can be used to elect right-minded Christians onto school boards by not declaring their agenda until after the election. They have been successful according to Simonds' *President's Report* of 1992.

> Our CEE chapters are finding outstanding school board candidates and teaching them how to get elected to office.... Everyday we are still hearing of great school board election victories in CEE chapter districts.... That makes over 1,250 NEW school board members in November 1991 elections. Our goal for November 1992 was 2,000—now we're going for 3,000 Christians NEWLY elected on school boards.

While I can applaud these groups for participating actively in civic life and can even agree that religions should be taught in schools, I do not condone the politicization of schools around a closed conservative Christian fear of difference. Conservative Christian fundamentalist groups and the Republican politicians who seek their votes recognize the connections between social institutions and their lives and act to ensure that their view will not be ignored. Their approach is instructive to other groups who may choose to participate actively in public life. They are highly organized, literate, connected, timely, persistent, and creative. They use petitions, letter campaigns, boycotts, and elections to make their points. Although they often seem to resort to oversimplification, outright distortion, and hyperbole, they attempt to articulate an economic, political, and moral argument to explain why schooling is important and why their vision of it will improve life in America. Their actions invite others to become active in civic life also.

Despite Reverend Falwell's reading of American history, the U.S. Constitution and the writings that surround it suggest that the state cannot favor one religion over others. This law against established state religion has frightened most teachers away from the study of religions as schools of thought and as important parts of history. However, you cannot understand much politics or history—the English in Ireland, Israel's West Bank, India's north/south conflict, or the boundary disputes between the Mohawk nation and New York and Ontario—unless you have some sense of the religious systems involved. Unless religions are part of the curriculum, we cannot hope to foster the rights, responsibilities, and respect for the religious differences in the world, our nation, and local communities. Religion is an important difference we must address when we consider how we wish to live together.

However, I must talk back to conservative Christian fundamentalists when they try to remake schools in their own image. They play on people's fear of difference rather than help them to understand where differences come from and how we can see diversity as a strength. When former Reagan speechwriter and conservative media pundit Pat Buchanan calls for "culture wars," he is not hoping to bring harmony to America in any other way than the elimination or subjugation of abnormal Americans. The "stealth" elections of conservative Christian fundamentalists to school boards is a dishonest ploy to hone school curricula, texts, personnel, and practices according to a paranoia that ultimately would stifle difference, deny rights, and destroy real patriotism, freedom, and justice.

Will critical literacy education end students' childhood by exposing them to the seamier sides of society before they are capable or ready to handle them as some naturalist educators charge? Do critical perspectives politicize schools by imposing a fixed agenda upon children? I think not, but I can understand why some might see it that way. The confusion, I believe, comes from an ahistorical view of childhood and an inconsistent gaze upon imposition.

Childhood is a social category, not a biological or even a psychological fact. In *Centuries of Childhood* (1962, Random) Philippe Aries explains that the category of childhood as we know it did not even exist in the West before the fifteenth and sixteenth centuries. During the Middle Ages children were mixed with adults as soon as they were considered capable of doing without their mothers. Although this may not seem to be the ideal circumstances for young people, it does attest to the historical relativity of the idea of childhood.

During the early seventeenth century, American children had a critical economic function—they were a vital part of the family laborforce. While adults were deeply concerned about young people's religious and moral welfare, there were no institutions except the church designed to assist parents in these matters. With changes in commerce and industry, middle-class families began to view children as consumers rather than producers in the economy. Since not all men would be farmers and not all women would be wives, schools took on a greater interest in young people's preparation for life. Children of families with lesser economic means continued to enter the workforce whenever able. In cities, however, it was not always possible to find work, and as families felt the economic and social strains of urbanization and industrialization, many urban families fell apart, leaving homeless and destitute children. As early as 1825 the New York House of Refuge provided the same services for children as the workhouse did for the adult destitute. By 1850, the Children's Aid Society was sweeping children off city streets and shipping them off to waiting western families to become vital parts of those families' economies. During the twentieth century, changes in economic conditions warranted federal legislative answers to child labor, poverty, and homelessness. Yet all three problems still exist for many American children.

The evolution of the idea of childhood has been more complex for females, immigrants, Native Americans, African Americans, Latinos, and the children of other groups. For them, life has also been mediated by biases toward gender, race, and social class. For example, female children were only recently considered capable of socialization for nonmenial paid work. African and African American children endured two hundred years of slavery and an additional one hundred years of social apartheid. Many Native American children still must separate themselves from their family in order to attend school, although the curriculum less often attempts to suppress native cultures and languages. Even these qualifications disregard ethnic, language, or regional variations in the notion of childhood.

In this historical light, what do critics mean when they charge that critical educators won't let children be children? I believe they are perpetuating a romanticized and nostalgic view of childhood, most noticeably a middle- and upper-class white male version in which children are all sweetness and light. While I can stretch my childhood into one of these fantasies, I now realize that it came on the backs of both my father, who started work in a lumber camp at eleven years old driving draft horses, and of my mother, who was raised and able to forego paid work to make a home. We had apples and grapes because migrant families came every September to pick them from orchards in our county and the ones to the west and from vineyards in the counties south of us. We had milk and corn because farm families worked from early morning until after dinner in our township. We had clothes and heat because families worked in fields, mills, and mines in the states south of New York.

To "remember" this idyllic childhood, I must forget the Korean and the Vietnam wars, bomb shelters, and the negative reactions to the civil rights and women's movements. I must overlook the ethnic bias that forced us to fight with children from other ethnic groups in and around our town. I must ignore the separation of the kids whose families owned their houses from those that rented in our neighborhood, and the alcohol abuse of fathers and my teenage friends. To believe in such a childhood, I must deny that I was a conscious, living being in spite of what I saw on *Ozzie and Harriet*, *Leave It to Beaver*, or *The Donna Reed Show*. On whose backs and through what amnesia shall we let today's middle- and upper-class white young people remain children? As journalist Alex Kotlowitz (1992, Doubleday) suggests in the title of his book on two boys growing up in a public housing project in Chicago, *There Are No Children Here.*

Some critics of critical perspectives charge that critical educators impose their politics on students. At first glance, this concern may appear legitimate. True imposition is the hallmark of politicized education. I agree that children's lives and classroom practices should not be politicized. Yet this charge and its underlying concern are left unidentified or completely ignored in much of children's lives and in schools. Although far from presenting a unified position, popular culture, the media, advertisements, and schools direct children to construct certain identities for themselves. Perhaps an anecdote will help make this point about who is imposing what on whom and with what effect.

While attempting critical literacy education in a first grade classroom in Duluth, Minnesota, twenty-eight six-year-olds and I struck on the theme of studying toys. During our brainstorming about types and names of toys, one fellow responded to a question about an Easy Bake Oven by declaring disapprovingly, "That's a girl's toy." Not one to let such a fat pitch go by, I followed up with, "What's a girl's toy? Are there other girls' toys listed on the board?" Although they couldn't read all the names I had listed, the boys were quite adept at labeling toys according to gender. The most basic girl's toy I was told is "a doll." And the most basic doll for a six-year-old, apparently, is a Barbie doll, a toy which has been around since I was a kid.

"How do you know that Barbies are for girls? I know that there's Ken and that he has a little brother named Kevin. Aren't they for boys?" I asked. The unanimous conclusion was that they had only seen girls playing with Barbies on television and in their neighborhoods, and no boy would admit to having received a doll as a present. Because the girls weren't doing much talking beyond naming all of Barbies' friends that you could buy, I asked them to "Tell me about Barbie" The girls listed her attributes—stiffness (only one joint per limb), an inability to stand (feet made for high heels), lots of hair (although Barbies are always blond, Barbie's friends have many different hair colors), and small heads. This discussion quickly expanded to Barbie's accessories, which began a deluge of desires for all the things that the girls hoped to buy or, rather, have bought for them. These items are advertised on television, in *Barbie* magazine, on the back of Barbie cards, and in Barbie comic books. Many of them had domestic connotations—kitchens, tea sets, bridal gowns, and so on. But just as many put Barbie in the fast lane—sports cars, pool furniture, and safari wear.

Just before my time was up for that week, I declared that all of the descriptions of Barbie reminded me of G. I. Joe and his combative comrades. As a group, these figures are stiff, plastic, single jointed, can't stand up easily, and have lots of accessories. "They seem like dolls to me," I said, and then the lesson was over. Before we began a week later, a boy approached me and stated, "My father said that G. I. Joes are not dolls. They are action figures." "Where do you think your father found that name for G. I. Joes?" "We saw it on TV." Fortunately, I had videotaped Barbie and G. I. Joe commercials from morning cartoon shows, and we continued our analysis of boy and girl toys and how they compared by examining these tapes. In the end, we decided that children had to bring the story to Barbies and G. I. Joes because "they're really just like hangers by themselves." That is, children (their parents, relatives, and friends) must buy things to hang on them or to place around them in order for children to engage in fantasy play with them. The dolls are cheap, but the accessories, which never stop changing, are five to ten dollars per item.

Through the dialogue about toys and commercials, we revealed the politicization of children's everyday lives in ways that have specific consequences for their construction of identities. The politics and sociology of toys encourages boys to see themselves as loud, aggressive, and rugged and girls to see themselves as domestic, narcissistic, and passive. The only characteristic that boys and girls are to share apparently is materialism—they both are to be avid consumers. To me this is an imposition of sexism, racism, and classism on children because these toys are gendered, race is portrayed negatively in G. I. Joes and is ignored in Barbies, and the accumulation of things is celebrated. The boys' reluctance to discuss girl toys, the girls' reluctance to speak at all until the topic was Barbies, and the parent who would not allow his son to consider the possibility of playing with dolls all suggest that these impositions affect our understanding of ourselves and color our relationships with others.

Not everyone accepts this imposition, of course. For example, recently a group of adults calling themselves the BLO (Barbie Liberation Organization) switched the voice tapes for "talking" Barbies and G. I. Joes in several department stores in New Jersey and New York. The lucky consumers who bought these dolls heard Barbie rant, "Eat lead, Cobra" and G. I. Joe chirp, "I can't wait to get married." A true story!

Dress codes, required reading lists, classroom routines, and learning competitions in their many forms all impose adult political views on children. They all provide experiences for children from which they are to construct their identities— their self-concepts, concepts of others, and beliefs about human relationships. Of course, educators and parents put them in place to do just that.

Therefore, to provide children with opportunities to read these and other texts critically is not an extraordinary imposition. Critical literacy education is a necessary part of learning to participate actively in civic life; that is, to identify, name, and act upon the impositions of everyday life. Perhaps the injustices in our lives continue unabated because too many Americans have constructed identities that accept the impositions of racial, gender, and social class biases, competitiveness, and war as facts of life without stopping to ask why things are the way they are, who benefits from these conditions, and how can we make them more equitable. Critical literacy education, then, is not a politicized imposition that young and old people must accept. Rather, it is a tool they can use to deconstruct the walls that separate the few who can build mansions from the many who can build only dreams. Critical literacy is a tool to construct more open and honest identities and more equitable and just communities.

The belief that rationality leads to freedom has been a central tenet of liberalism for centuries. To be free, individuals must become more aware of themselves, their relationship with society, and the world around them. This liberating notion has guided scientists as they promote an order to the universe, and it is the foundation of the empirical research movement in American education. According to its advocates, once educators and parents are aware of the available choices among methods and the research support for each, they will free themselves from the haphazard progress of subjective methods of instruction that inhibit personal and social progress.

This belief clearly resonates when educators evoke the phrase "and I have the research to prove it." This phrase is meant to close discussion over possible goals, plausible interpretations of events, or alternative ways of acting. Once the research card has been played, all other participants are expected to fold their hands in the name of science and freedom because science is believed to be value-free and nonpartisan and is supposed to make the decisions for people. Yet this is not often the case. Typically, values and vested interests get in the way. For example, during the 1980s many reading researchers examined school textbooks because those texts directed most teacher and student activities during most lessons. The results of the research showed that textbooks were poorly organized, difficult to read, and necessarily dated in content and instructional suggestions. If science alone were to decide what ought to be done in classrooms, then we'd expect that researchers would suggest that teachers free themselves from textbooks and conduct their lessons using whatever materials would aid their actions. Equally important, this research-based rationality would also free students from the frustrating experience of trying to make sense of incomprehensible and inaccurate textbooks. While these suggestions should be expected, they are not what happened. Instead of freeing teachers and students, researchers used the scientific findings to direct their comments to textbook publishers, telling them how to improve their wares in order to make textbook-driven instruction more effective and tying teachers and students more tightly to textbooks. This research and its subsequent use by researchers was neither liberating nor value-free. Rather, it was used to further psychological and cultural literacy educational perspectives.

Problems also arise when several sides in a discussion have research to back up their position. For example, how should urban educators proceed in helping students learn to be literate? Should they teach preschoolers and parents to crack the code according to state-of-the-science reading instruction? Should they recognize that opportunities to construct literacy are more constrained in traditional schooling than in students' homes and adopt appropriate methods? Or should they recognize that literacy learning is directly tied to economic and social opportunity and develop methods that simultaneously expand urban students' and adults' social and economic opportunities while supporting their literacy development?

Your answer, of course, depends on the assumptions and goals on which you will base your action. Each of the questions I posed above for urban educators are research based, but each set of research took different forms and was directed toward different ends. The research base for the first question is most likely psychological in nature, comparing alternative interventions in students' reading development. The second question is based on naturalistic research that took place over long periods of time. Researchers came to understand how the patterns of interaction in homes differed from those at school. The last question is based on critical studies in which the context of the research base for the second question was broadened beyond the two settings both in space and time. If different educators followed the implied direction in these questions, they would take children, schools, and society toward different futures.

If many positions are research based, then how shall we decide which way to go? One possible solution is to line up the research findings in order to let them compete with one another to see who is telling the best truth. However, since advocates of each position strive toward different goals, a fair or useful competition is virtually impossible. Research competitions among different points of view leave us where we started, asking whose truth is really real. I think we must acknowledge that science by itself cannot determine how we should act as educators. That is, we should renounce the belief that science will direct our lives automatically without our having to make difficult choices about what we value and how we wish to live together. In some respects, we have already made this decision concerning medical care, the environment, economics, and many other fields. We now know that science has not made us free or carefree in these areas. I'm not trying to say that research is useless. Instead, there are limits to scientists' ability to inform us and to set us free. As sociologist C. Wright Mills wrote in *The Sociological Imagination*,

> Freedom is not merely the chance to do as one pleases; neither is it merely the opportunity to choose between set alternatives. Freedom is, first of all, the chance to formulate the available choices, to argue over them—and then the opportunity to choose. That is why freedom cannot exist without an enlarged role of human reason in human affairs.

To direct our choices and our human reason, we must dispense with claims that scientific "truth" transcends the particulars of the context and community in which we find ourselves and that we must replace those claims with a desire for solidarity within that context and community. That is, we should determine our direction as educators, as parents, as human beings by our answers to questions of how we wish to live together. With that goal, however temporal it may be, we can choose some explanations, theories, or stories and dismiss others when the former produce our desired community better than the latter. Then we can stand on our belief that not everything that "works" is desirable; that not every belief that is "true" is to be acted upon, and that some scientifically successful approaches will work at cross-purposes with our goals. Those that do not align themselves with our goals are irrelevant to our work. For example, urban kids may be able to be taught to crack the code by second grade using learning competitions or may profit from blending home and school patterns of interaction, but these scientific "facts" do not necessarily help them to become critically literate, active in civic life, more understanding of themselves and others, or less afraid of difference and cooperation. If these are our goals, then those scientific findings are less important.

Values and visions about how we wish to live together with our differences must precede our search for descriptions, theories, explanations, and stories. Our choices about what to research and how to go about it are conditioned by where we hope to go in the broadest sense. Our ideas about values, aesthetics, politics, and normal behavior and preferences are integral to educational research, its interpretation, and its utilization. Science and research cannot determine or validate these values, visions, or ideas. Science and research can only be used to help us develop effective methods for working toward our values, visions, and ideas.

Most often when someone says, "I have the research to prove it," they are caught up in the power of research and science to explain what they value, as if that were reality, without looking to the consequences of their findings on the communities within which we must live. We can use research from psychological perspectives to make children crack the code or from naturalistic perspectives to approximate sophisticated literacies right from the start. For that matter, we can make them adopt normal American values and characteristics as well as they are able. But what price must we pay for these approaches and toward what ends will they lead us? What

are the goals on which we will act and what are the consequences of those actions?

Just like its advocates, critical literacy education is not a
complete position. It does not have every theoretical or practical contingency worked out for all contexts. It is not beyond
reproach or questioning. Most teachers, parents, administrators, and students ask questions because of their own history
in schools. Even if they were unsuccessful in learning traditional academic lessons, most learned the procedural lessons
of schooling all too well. They learned that texts and teachers
are the ultimate authority concerning which knowledge is
valuable and which is not. They learned that accuracy is the
key to learning, regardless of content, and that error is as
much a moral failure as an academic one. They learned that
in order to learn something complex, they must master its
constituent parts in a proper sequence and then wait for tests
to determine whether or not they know anything of value.
Those who were successful at school attribute their success to
their capacity to master these procedural lessons as well as the
content presented. Those who failed the tests complained
about the content, perhaps, but they internalized the blame
for their failure, believing that they had not worked at it ear-
nestly enough.

Critical literacy education challenges every facet of these
thoughts and beliefs about schooling. As prisoners of their
own educational history, most people ask sincere questions in
legitimate attempts to understand these challenges. For those
questions and people, I have great respect and hope we can
use your inquiries to establish dialogues that will improve our
chances of finding equitable and just ways to live together.
However, to those who ask insincere questions in order to
protect privilege and hide its consequences, I'll continue to
talk back.

And if I'd any time left in my allotted ten minutes to
respond during that Thursday night lecture, I would have
told those two hundred teachers, parents, administrators, and
the three other speakers just one more story.

Afterword

*W*hen I was born my father was already in his fifties. Until he died when I was twenty-three, he appeared to not age at all because he always seemed so old to me. Because he had to go to work as a boy, he protected me from labor until I was fifteen and incorrigible at school and at home. Through his friends, he found three jobs "to keep me busy," as he said. I was a grocery bagger at a local market on Tuesdays and Fridays after school until 8 P.M.; I unloaded boxcars full of retaining wall ties, peat moss, and such for a landscaping company on Mondays, Wednesdays, and Thursdays from 4 to 7; and I mucked one hundred stalls at a standardbred horse farm every Saturday and Sunday. For the six months or so before my father told the grocery and landscaping company that I was under the legal working age, I tasted what it must have been like for my father when he was young. Of course, I could escape to school each weekday and could sleep in my own bed and not share a bunk in a loggers' barracks.

This experience brought me closer to my father, and I began to take new interest in the stories he told about his life. For instance, I learned that my grandfather was famous throughout the Adirondack Mountains for his size (his nickname was Babe), for his prodigious drinking and bad business judgment, and for stomping a bear to death that had treed him while he was topping trees for logging (my father had a newspaper clipping of this event). I learned that at age eight, my father skipped school to be the unofficial doorman at the grand opening of Woolworth's in Watertown, New York, until he unknowingly patted his Aunt Mary on the backside while saying, "Go ahead on in, now," to all the customers. Among many other things, I learned that he had helped to organize upstate New York fruit truckers during the 1920s. "I was the one who stood behind the little Jew and punched my hand until each man signed a union card," he told me.

From my father's stories, I learned that he was human, full of dreams his whole life, and also full of contradictions. Over the years, his stories have become my stories for better and worse. I, too, am incomplete, a dreamer, and fraught with inconsistencies. I have many more questions than answers, more hope than is healthy, and more struggles ahead in learning to deal with human difference on a daily basis. So many of our everyday habits are sexist, racist, and classist without our conscious attention or intention. At times, I cling to my father's stories to remember who I am, what I come from, and where I intend to go. While I have my own stories to tell, they are attached to those of my father as I try to decide which traits I hope to continue and which I hope to extinguish in my life.

Laura and Tim-Pat mirror my inconsistencies as they learn to deal with my stories as well as their own. From the frilly dresses in Laura's closet to Tim-Pat's X Men, Ninja Turtles, and Vikings, they move between stories that reproduce the status quo and those that challenge it. What distinguishes their struggle for identity from my own is the critical literacy education in which we are currently engaged. They listen to and read many more stories from different and varied sources than the standard, normal American stories of my youth. For example, when they hear anyone can grow up to be president, they know that this has been true only for white men of means. They know that these standard stories do not typically apply to themselves, their family, or friends. This knowledge does not defeat them. On the contrary, it empowers them to see through the rhetoric of American myths to the realities of their lives. They realize that to accept those myths uncritically is to limit their understanding of themselves and society and to reduce the possibilities of creating new ways in which we can live together with our differences. Because of their education, the volume of those myths and standard stories is much softer in their heads than it is in mine.

Tim-Pat and Laura have learned to listen for the silences in standard stories—for what's not said and for who isn't allowed to speak for themselves. They realize that who is telling their stories is just as important as what that story is about. Kathleen, their teachers, and I work to ensure that those silences do not continue in their lives and stories. We want them to hear John Brown, Jane Addams, W. E. B. DuBois, Septima Clark, Holly Near, and Daniel Shays tell their stories as points of comparison with the stories of Neto Villareal, Norvell Smith, Beni Seballos, and Linda Warsaw and other young contemporary North American activists. By connecting others' stories of the past and present with their own, they push to explore how these stories and the lives they represent interact, support, and subordinate one another. At home and during school, they have at times begun to understand that they have the ability, the right, and the responsibility to tell their stories, to listen to others, and to act upon their new knowledge to promote equity and justice. In this way, the diverse stories and the environments in which they hear, tell, and act upon them have direct consequences for their construction of their civic and personal identities.

Critical literacy education, then, must enable those who have been silenced to tell their stories and those who have been privileged in school and society to tell theirs in different ways. Through question-centered curriculum, dialogue around issues of difference, and participation in civic life, we learn to see ourselves as fully participating members of communities in and out of schools. This part of our identities makes us see the world differently, makes us tell different stories, and makes us different human beings. For when we tell or listen—write or read—our stories and consider how ours fit with the stories other lives tell, we can no longer be complacent about the inequalities and injustices that envelop our schools and society. We cannot remain silent about the standard stories and their consequences for the construction of our identities, for the way we live, and for people's lives throughout the world.

And of course this reminds me of another story—one my father repeated often during my adolescence. He claimed to be the first college graduate in his family. He'd smirk when he'd begin because he realized that his listeners knew that he left school in the fifth grade. However, he had attended the Brookwood Labor College for two weeks on a scholarship to discuss the union campaign for truckers. His jokes about which fraternity he pledged, his football scholarship, and his graduation with honors would turn serious when he reported that he studied with A. J. Muste, the famous labor, civil rights, and peace activist. My father believed Muste to be a great man and quoted him to me from time to time when I was unsure of myself, confused about what to do, and worried that I didn't have every detail worked out ahead of time. Only a few of those quotes stuck with me, but one of them is ringing in my ears right now: "Make up your mind and act, while your actions might make a difference!" It's still good advice.

Bibliographic Essay

The basic data for this book come from stories of my life as a student, teacher, and parent. I offer these stories and explanations as a reaction to the typical ways in which education, schooling, teaching, literacy, and children are considered. Usually, education is thought to be a synonym for schooling, teaching is treated as the transmission of information from authority to pupils' minds, literacy is limited to the ability to read and write print, and children are simultaneously characterized as the hope of the future and the bane of our existence. The stories I've told in *text, lies, & videotape* challenge those conceptualizations and offer different ways of thinking about our past, present, and future and how they relate to education.

Life stories fascinate me and have helped me to understand and connect with other people and the social structure that surrounds our lives in ways that so-called facts and figures have not and, perhaps, cannot. For example, reading the life stories in Stud Terkel's *Working* (1985, Ballentine) and *Hard Times* (1986, Pantheon), I've come to understand my father better as well as other people who lived through the Great Depression and constructed their lives accordingly. Watching *Strangers in Good Company* (1992, Touchstone) has helped me know my mother and women of her generation. My efforts to grasp the immigrant experience were greatly aided by reading Hamilton Holt's *The Life Stories of Undistinguished Americans* (1989, Routledge) and Maxine Hong Kingston's *China Men,* (1989, Random). Race relations became clearer with Derrick Bell's *Faces at the Bottom of the Well* (1993, Basic), Alex Kotlowitz's *There Are No Children Here* (1991, Doubleday), and Melissa Fay Green's *Praying for Sheetrock* (1991, Addison-Wesley). I am coming to understand the relationships of working people, race, and immigration with education and schooling by reading the stories in Myles Horton and Paulo Freire's dialogue book *We Make the Road by Walking* (1990, Temple University) and watching *Flirting* (1990, Warner Bros.). Life stories are a potent way of knowing.

Teachers' stories attracted me to teaching in the first place. Although I did not know any practicing teachers when I was twenty-four years old, I read the stories in Sylvia Ashton Warner's *Teacher* (1986, Touchstone), Herbert Kohl's *36 Children* (1988, Dutton) and Jonathan Kozol's *Death at an Early Age* (1985, Dutton) and decided that I wanted to be an elementary school teacher. Those stories have sustained me through several sets of second thoughts about that decision. I'm still drawn to teacher narratives and narratives about teachers. For example, Samuel Freeman's *Small Victories*, (1991, Harper Collins) Mike Rose's *Lives on the Boundary*, (1990, Viking) and even Pat Conroy's fictional *The Water is Wide* (1987, Bantam) have enabled me to see education in new ways. The stories in Kathleen Casey's *I Answer with My Life* (1993, Routledge) connect me with women teachers working for social change, and Vivian Paley's stories about her life with preschoolers—*Bad Guys Don't Have Birthdays* (1991, University of Chicago); *White Teacher* (1979, Harvard University); and *You Can't Say You Can't Play* (1992, Harvard University Press) challenge me to read the stories before me on a daily basis.

Stories connect me with "the other," people who often are not well represented in the typical discussions of education and schooling. Maxine Greene's *The Dialectic of Freedom* (1988, Teachers College) suggests that stories are one way that women can move from the private to the public in order to be heard. Valerie Polakow's *Lives on the Edge* (1993, University of Chicago) tells stories of the feminization of poverty and of the fastest growing impoverished group: children. The Children's Defense Fund's (1991) *The State of America's Children* supports these stories with facts and figures. In *Beyond Silenced Voices* (1993, SUNY) Lois Weis and Michelle Fine present stories of action taken to increase the chances that women and people of color participate in the decision making of public life in and out of schools. Janet Miller in *Creating Spaces and Finding Voices* (1990, SUNY), F. Michael Connelly and D. Jean Clandinin in *Teachers as Curriculum Planners* (1988, Teachers College) and Sue Middleton in *Educating Feminists* (1993, Teachers College) discuss the importance of life stories in teacher education. In each case, the storytellers set the stories of their lives within theoretical contexts that help direct their interpretations because our lives do not and cannot speak for themselves.

Stories, then, provide an important source of data about education, schooling, teaching, literacy, and children. Ann Berthoff wrote in *The Making of Meaning* (1981, Boynton-Cook), that stories examined theoretically are a form of research because "we do not need new information, we need to think about the information we have" (31), an idea first posed in C. Wright Mills' *The Sociological Imagination* (1959, Oxford University). Andrew Gitlin's *Teachers' Voices for School Change* (1991, Teachers College), Carol Witherell and Nel Nodding's *Stories Lives Tell* (1991, Teachers College), and Daniel McLaughlin and William Tierney's *Naming Silenced Lives* (1993, Routledge) offer details about how research on life stories can lead to social action:

> Individual memory must be preserved not simply for some romantic future where people will be able to see how we lived in the late twentieth century, but rather, we collect life stories as a way to document how we live now so that we might change how we live now. (McLaughlin and Tierney, 1993, 4).

Our lives and telling stories about our lives matter.

Stories represent our thoughts about what the world has been, what it is, and what it should become. What we make of the stories we tell and listen to depends on our theoretical beliefs about the world and how it works. Of course, not everyone agrees about the past, present, and future, and we have story representations for many sets of beliefs. Because schooling is positioned as a central institution in our society, the struggle over which stories best represent schooling burns intensely. The recent retreat from federal and state funding of public schools has thrown fuel on this fire. Apparently, everyone is discouraged about the prospects of schools in general, and everyone has a solution.

For example in *Educational Policy for a Pluralistic Democracy* Mark Holmes (1989, Falmer) tells the story of the abandonment of the scientific, psychological foundation of schools through discussions of charts and experimental studies. His stories offer increased academic planning and accountability based on verifiable scientific conclusions as the solution to schools' problems. Edward Fiske in *Smart Schools/Smart Kids* (1991, Touchstone) tells the stories of schools that have followed Holmes's advice. Lauren Resnick's *Education and Learning to Think* (1987, National Academy) and Tracy Kidder's *Among Schoolchildren* (1990, Avon), present rationales for scientific solutions in very different ways. Resnick tells the story of an economic imperative that Americans learn to think for a living in order to keep our nation competitive in world markets. Kidder details the life of one teacher as she struggles to make sense of a multicultural student body whose lives do not conform to traditional school expectations. *Lean on Me* (1989, Warner Bros.) offers the extremes to which educators will take their efforts to bring conformity. Finally, Myron Lieberman's choice of titles for his new book tells a story in itself—*Public Education: An Autopsy* (1993, Harvard University).

Science is not the solution of choice for all stories about schooling. In *The Schools We Deserve*, Diane Ravitch (1987, Basic) argues that schools have lost sight of the best of academic traditions—separate subject areas and strict discipline—during the last forty years in our efforts to include more types of Americans in the same classrooms. Allan Bloom's *The Closing of the American Mind* (1988, Touchstone) suggests that this democratization of schools has ruined everyone's chances for academic excellence. *The Paideia Proposal* (1984, MacMillan) is Mortimer Adler's attempt to sketch the elementary and secondary school curriculum that he believes would reopen Americans' minds. This perspective is well represented in the *Dead Poet's Society* (1989, Touchstone) and *To Serve Them All My Days* (1981, BBC). Former Assistant Secretary of the Department of Education Chester Finn implores parents to find these arguments compelling in *We Must Take Charge: Our Schools and Our Future* (1993, Free); John Chubb and Terry Moe use selective facts and figures in *Politics, Markets, and American Schools* (1990, Brookings) to explain why federal and state school funding should be diverted to private schools in order to achieve academic excellence there while public schools remain democratic; and David Kearns and Denis Doyle set a "bold plan" for making American schools competitive in *Winning the Brain Race* (1991, ICS Press).

Since the psychological and the cultural perspectives have been most prevalent in American schools, there are several texts that attempt to identify their contradictions. For example, Mara Sapon Shevin argues in *Playing Favorites* (1994, SUNY) that gifted education disrupts classrooms and community in order to privilege primarily white middle- and upper-class students at the expense of the rest. *Little Man Tate* (1991, Orion), *Searching for Bobby Fischer* (1993, Orion), and even *Bull Durham* (1988, Orion) show differential education for talented individuals as problematic. *The Simpsons* (on Fox) and "Calvin and Hobbes" (Universal Press) lampoon traditional schooling on a regular basis.

Since the 1950s and Paul Goodman's *Growing Up Absurd* (1956, Vintage), Hollywood has poked fun at the isolation and futility of the ways high schools are organized. *Fast Times at Ridgemont High* (1982, Universal), *Pump Up the Volume* (1990, New Line), and *Heathers* (1988, New World) portray some of the problems adolescents face at school. My all time favorite critique of the cultural literacy perspective is *Bill and*

Ted's Excellent Adventure (1989, Orion) in which Bill and Ted time travel to bring back a living term paper in order to pass their history class.

In *Insult to Intelligence* (1988, Heinemann), Frank Smith tells the story of how too much of the wrong kind of psychology, of the artificial separation of subject matter, and of authoritarian control have made schools a bad place for children and adolescents to spend six or seven hours daily. Ron Miller asks *What Are Schools For?* (1990, Holistic Education) and answers his own question with a single word: children. *Teachers* (1984, CBS/Fox) offers a critique of both the psychological and cultural perspectives as it presents the story of a teacher trying to overcome the bureaucracy of schooling to focus on his students. Caroline Pratt's *I Learn from Children* (1948, Harper Collins & Rowe) presents a historical treatment of the naturalistic solution to school problems through her story of forty years as head teacher at the City and Country School in New York City. John Holt's classic account of *How Children Fail* (1988, Delacorte) is a must-read for everyone. *The Sandlot* (1993, 20th Century Fox) shows how children teach themselves when the opportunity presents itself. Advocates for creating schools with children at their center revel in the stories in Eleanor Duckworth's *Having Wonderful Ideas and Other Essays on Teaching and Learning* (1987, Teachers College). Arnold Schwarzenegger presents a recent satire of the naturalistic perspective in *Kindergarten Cop* (1990, Universal).

Although all of the above stories are important and useful to gain perspective on the struggle over schooling, the most compelling stories to me come from advocates of a critical perspective on schooling. Jonathan Kozol's telling in *Savage Inequalities* (1992, HarperCollins) paints a portrait of the continuation of racial and economic apartheid in this country—forty years after the Supreme Court ruled that separate but equal schools are unconstitutional. Stanley Aronowitz and Henry Giroux's *Education Still Under Siege* (1993, Bergin & Garvey) describes the consequences of the continued pursuit of scientific, academic, and naturalistic nonsolutions to the problems of schooling in the United States. Ira Shor in *Critical Teaching and Everyday Life* (1987, University of Chicago), William Ayers in *To Teach* (1993, Teachers College) and Kathleen Weiler in *Women Teaching for Change* (1987, Bergin & Garvey), offer personal stories of teachers working for equality and justice. Ann Bastian's *Choosing Equality* (1986, Temple University), and Jesse Goodman's *Elementary Schooling for Critical Democracy* (1992, SUNY) explain the policies and theory behind democratic schools, and George Wood's *Schools That Work* (1992, Dutton) and the various publications of the Rethinking Schools group (1001 E. Keefe, Milwaukee, WI 53212) present stories of teachers, students, and parents attempting to live and work in democratic schools and communities. Films such as *True Believer* (1989, Columbia) and *Miles from Home* (1988, Cinecon) offer examples that move education beyond schooling as the protagonists learn about the roles that race, gender, and social class play in actively participating in public life.

Stories about schooling and education include references to the debate about how literacy is learned and taught in and around schools. Jeanne Chall's *The Reading Crisis* (1990, Harvard University), Marilyn Adams' *Beginning to Read* (1990, MIT), and Rudolph Flesch's *Why Johnny Still Can't Read* (1983, HarperCollins) offer the psychological stories. E. D. Hirsch in *Cultural Literacy* (1988, Random) and *Fundamentals of Good Education Series* (Random), Neil Postman in *Teaching as a Conserving Activity* (1987, Dell), and Bruno Bettelheim and Karen Zelan in *On Learning to Read* (1982, Random) present stories about how reading and writing were once taught and why they should be taught that way again to benefit ourselves and our country and civilization. The naturalistic approach to literacy learning is retold in various ways in Frank Smith's *Reading Without Nonsense* (1985, Teachers College); Jerome Harste, Virginia Woodward, and Carolyn Burke's *Language Stories and Literacy Lessons* (1984, Heinemann); and Donald Graves' *Experimenting with Writing* Heinemann) series.

Because advocates of naturalistic perspectives on literacy recognize that who's telling the story is equally as important as the story being told, there are many collections of educators' firsthand accounts of literacy learning written for various audiences. For example, Glenda Bissex's *GYNS AT WRK* (1980, Harvard University) reports her son's literacy development. Kathleen Shannon's *At Home at School* (1994, The Wright Group) chronicles her and Laura's first few months of dealing with schools and literacy expectations. Sondra Perl and Nancy Wilson's *Through Teachers' Eyes* (1986, Heinemann) represents teachers' work in collaboratively written stories. Jane Hansen, Thomas Newkirk, and Donald Graves in *Breaking Ground* (1985, Heinemann) and Judith Newman in *Finding Our Own Way* (1989, Heinemann) collect teachers' stories about changing the ways to teach reading and writing. Newman turns her gaze onto her own teaching in *Interwoven Conversations* (1991, Heinemann) joining Nancy Atwell's *In the Middle* (1987, Boynton-Cook), Linda Rief's *Seeking Diversity* (1992, Heinemann), *La Lectrese* or *The Reader* (1990, Orion), and Carol Avery's . . . *And with a Light Touch* (1993, Heinemann) as extended first-person narratives about teaching and literacy.

Advocates of a critical perspective identify contradictions within psychological, cultural, and naturalistic perspectives. For example, in *Broken Promises* (1989, Bergin & Garvey), I discuss how psychological perspectives on reading have been adopted by the government and business to standardize reading theory and teaching in ways that prevent students' access to sophisticated forms of literacy. Allan Luke's *Literacy, Textbooks, and Ideology* (1988, Falmer) and Michael Apple's *Teachers and Text* (1988, Routledge) explain the rationales for and encoding of normal American values and morals into the structure, content, and language of textbooks, excluding most students' lives from consideration during school hours. The most coherent critiques of naturalistic literacy education come from Australia. The essays in Bill Green's *The Insistence of the Letter* (1993, Falmer) suggest theoretical ties between the heretofore separate psychological and naturalistic perspectives. In Bill Cope and Mary Kalantzis's *The Powers of Literacy* (1993, Falmer), various writers challenge the possibilities of naturalistic perspectives on education as a tool for working-class children to succeed in schools and in life. They argue that because naturalistic educators attempt to treat all students as equals, past inequalities are allowed to continue in and out of the classroom.

Denny Taylor and Catherine Dorsey-Gaines in *Growing Up Literate* (1988, Heinemann), examine working-class and primarily African American efforts to develop literacy. I defy anyone to remain dry-eyed as they recount the assigned minute-to-minute behaviors of Shauna's day at school. Susan Phillips shows how Native Americans can be forced to become *The Invisible Culture* (1982, Longman) through the official definition of literacy and the consequent actions of teachers. In *Ways with Words* (1984, Cambridge University), Shirley Brice Heath demonstrates how students from different social groups bring different literacies with them to school, and how schools honor only the varieties that middle- and upper-class students bring. Sandra Hollingsworth describes a group of teachers' efforts to overcome structural biases in literacy definitions and teaching practices in *Teacher Research and Urban Literacy Education* (1994, Teachers College).

These critiques and studies require a more expansive definition of literacy than the ones typically offered by advocates of psychological, cultural, and naturalistic perspectives. Paulo Freire and Donaldo Macedo suggest in *Literacy* (1989, Bergin & Garvey) that literacy is being able to read the word and the world. In their view, literacy has the potential to enable literate beings to interrogate the texts they encounter and the social relations that those texts represent. They argue that literacy has the potential to raise society's have-nots into a critical consciousness so that they no longer consider themselves to be "Objects" that cultural and economic elites can manipulate at will. Rather, as these have-nots become literate, they see themselves as culture beings—"Subjects"—in the decision making that affects their lives. In *With Literacy and Justice for All* (1991, Falmer), Carole Edelsky explains that

> the difference between the literate person as an Object and as Subject is social and political, not individual. It requires a look at who else is involved and how, and at the role and power of the literate in relation to the role and power of the other(s). Ultimately, it refers to the amount of control a person has over the print-use and the conduct of the literacy event. (76)

In *The Struggle to Continue* (1990, Heinemann), I attempt to flesh out the history of the development of this conceptualization of literacy in the United States. James Gee discusses in *Social Linguistics and Literacies* (1991, Falmer) how apparently individual practices such as reading are really social practices in which social groups speak to each other through individuals. *Critical Literacy* (1993, SUNY), edited by Colin Lankshear and Peter McLaren, provides theoretical possibilities for what this reconceptualization of literacy means for schooling and everyday life.

Critical literacy expands the traditional scope of literacy and the literate. David Trend in *Cultural Pedagogy* (1992, Bergin & Garvey), discusses the need to read culture and cultural representations as well as print. In *Hard Bodies* (1994, Rutgers University), Susan Jeffords explains how to read film to determine how Hollywood influences male identity construction. Leslie Roman and others explore a similar argument through *Being Feminine: The Politics of Popular Culture* (1988, Falmer), which addresses the images of women and girls in advertisements, on television, around the music industry, and throughout romance novels. Douglas Noble ties the recent enthusiasm for computers and computer literacy to military intelligence research and argues that computer-assisted learning amounts to *The Classroom Arsenal* (1991, Falmer). *Reading Rodney King/Reading Urban Uprising* (1993, Routledge) edited by Robert Gooding-Williams, offers a collection of essays that demand that we recognize media manipulation of our understanding of the world and ourselves by the ways in which they control our access to alternative points of view on race and economics that challenge normal American values.

Race, gender, class, ethnicity, and language diversity are inextricably part of literacy. Theresa Perry and James Fraser collected essays for *Freedom's Plow* (1993, Routledge) including one by Lisa Delpit to demonstrate how race is a central feature of literacy and literature. *School Daze* (1988, Columbia), *Mississippi Masala* (1991, Columbia), and *Love Field* (1992, Orion) suggest the complexities of race relations and reading the social texts in and out of schools. In *Ain't No Makin' It* (1994, Westview), Jay Macleod tells the stories of the members of two high school gangs as they move into adulthood without many prospects of reaching the American dream or of developing their abilities to understand why they face social immobility. Films such as *Educating Rita* (1983, Columbia) and television programs such as *Roseanne* (ABC) demonstrate the love/hate relationships between the working classes and schooling, both the boredom and the hope. Outside of schooling, the desperate education of poverty is represented in *An American Heart* (1992, Warner Bros.) and *A Perfect World* (1993, Warner Bros.) with the toxic literacies of institutions that ensure the continuation of families in poverty. Pam Gilbert explores how girls are taught to be girls through the routines, procedures, and literature of literacy lessons in *Gender, Literacy, and the Classroom* (1986, Australian International Reading Association). Language, culture, and literacy are discussed in the context of Puerto Rican student experience in elementary schools in Catherine Walsh's *Pedagogy and the Struggle for Voice* (1990, Bergin & Garvey). Films like *The Joy Luck Club* (1993, Hollywood) and *Passion Fish* (1992, Miramax) demonstrate the intersections of race, ethnicity, class, and culture and their relationship to reading the world. Susan Rose tells stories about the struggle over the definition, process, and content of literacy education in the many censorship battles initiated by the religious Right in *Keeping Them Out of the Hands of Satan* (1990, Routledge).

To help children, adolescents, and adults develop critical literacy, Eleanor Kutz and Hephzibah Roskelly suggest you need *An Unquiet Pedagogy* (1991, Boynton-Cook). Henry Giroux calls it *Schooling and the Struggle for Public Life* (1989, University of Minnesota) in his theoretical justification for changing the rationale for schooling from developing workers to fit business' specifications to educating an active democratic citizenry set on justice and equality. Ira Shor brings *Freire in the Classroom* (1987, Boynton-Cook), Roger Simon suggests *Teaching Against the Grain* (1992, Bergin & Garvey) and I describe teachers *Becoming Political* (1992, Heinemann), while Deborah Britzman believes that *Practice Makes Practice* (1991, SUNY). In a pamphlet, Herb Kohl explains why so many working-class students and students of color resist education in *I Won't Learn from You* (1991, Milkweed). Jeanne Brady in *Schooling the Young* (1995, SUNY), expands this focus and presents examples from her own and others' elementary school experience. In *Feminism and Critical Pedagogy* (1992, Routledge), Carmen Luke and Jennifer Gore ask critical educators to be reflexive in their enthusiasm when developing such approaches to teaching.

From others' and from my own stories, I hope that educators and parents can read the partisan nature of education, the ideological practices in schools and traditional reading and writing programs, and the politicized intentions of currently popular calls for reform. Moreover, we can develop and engage in projects of possibility in and out of schools that will change the stories adults and children tell and write about their lives. In these new stories, we will represent our hopes, our dreams, and our actions to make this a better and more just and equitable world in which to live together.